REASON
AND HOPE

Selections from the Jewish Writings
of Hermann Cohen

REASON AND HOPE

Selections from the Jewish Writings of Hermann Cohen

Translated by EVA JOSPE

HEBREW UNION COLLEGE PRESS · CINCINNATI

Copyright 1971 by the B'nai B'rith Commission on Adult Education

Reprinted 1993 by the Hebrew Union College Press

Library of Congress Cataloging-in-Publication Data

Cohen, Hermann, 1842–1918.
    [Jüdische Schriften. English. Selections]
    Reason and hope : selections from the Jewish writings of Hermann
Cohen / translated, edited, and with an introduction by Eva Jospe.
        p. cm.
    Originally published: New York : Norton. [1971], in series: B'nai
B'rith Jewish heritage classics. With additional material.
    Includes bibliographical references.
    ISBN 0-87820-211-0
    1. Judaism. I. Jospe, Eva. II. Title.
BM45.C613 1993
296—dc20   93-7895
                                                                CIP

Printed on acid-free paper
Manufactured in the United States of America

". . . only the idea of God gives me the confidence
that morality will become reality on earth.
And because I cannot live without this confidence,
I cannot live without God."

Hermann Cohen

Contents

Preface

The contents of this Reader have been culled from the three volumes comprising Hermann Cohen's *Juedische Schriften* (Jewish Writings). The original essays were edited by Bruno Strauss and published posthumously, in 1924, in Berlin, with an introduction by Franz Rosenzweig, who had been Cohen's student and later became his personal friend.

The essays (together with lectures and letters of Jewish interest) range in scope from discussions of fundamental questions concerning the philosophy and ethics of Judaism and problems of Jewish education through treatises on the significance of Jewish holy days and interpretive investigations of traditional literary sources to issues of merely topical interest. Some of the discourses, addressed to an educated lay public, are somewhat popularized versions, others almost literal restatements of ideas Cohen had presented formally and on an academic level in his major Jewish work, *Die Religion der Vernunft* (The Religion of Reason).[1]

In preparing this volume, I have selected from Cohen's Jewish writings what seemed to me most representative of his thought as well as most likely to make a genuine contribution to our own religious thinking. Some of the selections are straight translations of an entire essay, others are excerpts from the original material. Square brackets in the text enclose editorial remarks, while parenthetic marks have either been taken over from the original or indicate quotation-sources.

Cohen, as Bruno Strauss mentions in his foreword to the

1. See Introduction.

Juedische Schriften, loved to refer to his own teaching as "sermon-izing," and was given to constant reiteration as a teacher and lecturer, in a conscious effort to drive a point home. Both these characteristics are much in evidence throughout the original. I have tried to eliminate, or at least reduce, some of the ponderous-ness of the author's style as well as his repetitiousness without cut-ting into the substance of his thought.

But while I have attempted to avoid unnecessary repetition, I have retained those I consider substantively necessary. To have edited them out would have meant to destroy what I intended to keep intact: the self-contained logic, inner coherence, and essential argument of any given essay or excerpt, so that it could be read and understood by itself. Moreover, Cohen's work is largely, and organically, built around certain themes of leit-motif import, and it is impossible to cut out all variations on those recurrent themes and still maintain the composition of the whole. Cross-references given in the footnotes should, however, call the reader's attention to, if not serve as a corrective for, some of the remaining repetitive-ness.

The Biblical quotes throughout the text have been taken, with their original spelling, from the Jewish Publication Society transla-tion of the Bible. But in some instances Cohen's German rendition of a Hebrew passage had to be translated literally because the argu-ment it illustrates rests on that particular rendition or paraphrase.

I should like to point out that the German terms *Einzigkeit* and *einzig*—of signal importance to and therefore reappearing through-out Cohen's writings on Judaism—have been variously rendered as uniqueness, unique Oneness, Oneness, singularity and, respec-tively, as the One and Only, the uniquely One or, simply, the One. This was done in an attempt to approximate as closely as possible certain subtle, contextually determined shades in the meaning of these two key concepts.

However, the wish to transmit to the English-speaking reader the precise meaning of these terms—which can be said to epitomize Hermann Cohen's entire philosophy of religion—has been much more than a mere matter of linguistic concern: in a larger sense, it has provided the motivation as well as the goal for this volume.

Lastly, I should like to express my warm appreciation to my husband, Alfred Jospe, who had originally suggested the preparation of this volume and its inclusion in the Jewish Heritage Classics Series, for his invaluable advice concerning many substantive and technical matters, and particularly for his assistance with the "Guide for Further Reading"; to Rabbi Zalman Schachter and David Calof, of the University of Manitoba, Canada, for their generous help in locating the sources of several obscure textual references; and to editors David Patterson and Lily Edelman for their close reading of the completed manuscript and their helpful suggestions.

Washington, D.C., April 1970   Eva Jospe

NOTE ON THE NEW PRINTING

This paperback edition of *Reason and Hope* appears more than twenty years after the book's first publication. Long out of print yet still much in demand, the volume has proven to be valuable for the college student and the lay reader interested in the Jewish writings of one of the leading and still highly influential Jewish thinkers of modern times. The Hebrew Union College Press is therefore pleased to make the book once again available. Aside from some additions to the "Further Readings" and a few corrections, it remains as in the first printing.

Thanks for assistance are due to Eva Jospe and to Theodore Wiener and for permission to reprint the volume to its original sponsors, the Commission on Adult Education of B'nai B'rith.

Introduction

Hermann Cohen was born in 1842, in the small German town of Coswig (Anhalt), the son of the traditional cantor and learned Hebrew teacher of the local Jewish congregation. His childhood was thus spent in an atmosphere of pious ritual observance and of regular Jewish study with his father, a practice so important to both father and son that they continued it even while the boy attended the *Gymnasium* in Dessau.

When barely fifteen, the youth became a student at the Jewish Theological Seminary in Breslau, then headed by Zacharias Frankel. In a reminiscence written in 1904, on the occasion of the Seminary's fiftieth anniversary, Cohen fondly recalls how Frankel used to impress upon his students the need to uphold the traditional religious framework of Judaism while applying the methods of science to its study. Among the young institution's illustrious teachers was Heinrich Graetz, under whom Cohen studied Talmud—to their mutual dissatisfaction, as implied in the latter's account of those days.

Cohen's most formative years coincided with a richly creative period in the intellectual life of German Jewry, and the young student was, directly or indirectly, influenced by men like Leopold Zunz, Abraham Geiger and Samson Raphael Hirsch. Yet at this point in his development, the world of the university and all it represented in the Germany of that era, and particularly his all-consuming interest in philosophy, proved stronger than his Jewish interests. He left the Seminary and, during the following years, attended the Universities of Breslau, Berlin and Halle, receiving his doctoral degree in 1865. Eventually, he went to Marburg Univer-

sity, where he lectured as a *Privatdozent* for only three years before being made a full professor, an unusual feat for a Jew at that
time. He taught at Marburg for forty years, from 1876 to 1912,
and became renowned as the founder and most prominent representative of the so-called neo-Kantian school of philosophy or,
simply, the Marburg School.[1]

As a Kant scholar, Cohen published several interpretive works
on the thought of that great German philosopher before he developed a system of his own. He called his philosophy "critical idealism" and expounded its theories in three works: *Logik der reinen
Erkenntnis* (Logic of Pure Knowledge), *Ethik des reinen Willens*
(Ethics of Pure Will), and *Aesthetik des reinen Gefuehls* (Aesthetics of Pure Feeling). A few years later, he wrote *Der Begriff
der Religion im System der Philosophie* (The Concept of Religion
within the System of Philosophy) which, dealing with the question
of the autonomy of religion, is an attempt to define the place of
religion within philosophy.

Despite his total immersion in the intellectual and cultural atmosphere of Marburg, Cohen never severed his ties with either
Judaism or Jewry, as did so many Jews who were members of the
German intelligentsia during that period and indeed until the rise
of Hitler. This is not to say that the young professor was particularly visible or audible in Jewish matters. In fact, his Jewish stance
appears to have been somewhat ambivalent, as evidenced by the
fact that of three essays he wrote on Jewish subjects in the 1860's,
only one was published at the time, a second anonymously, and a
third many years later.[2]

But in 1880 an incident occurred that turned Cohen into what,
in retrospect, he was to call a baal teshuvah (one who returns).
In that year, the eminent German historian Treitschke launched
an "academic" attack on Judaism. He denied Judaism's continued
spiritual significance, and thereby aroused Cohen's Jewish loyalties,

1. Other philosophers of the Marburg School include Paul Natorp, Ernst
   Cassirer, F.A. Lange and, initially, Nicolai Hartmann.
2. *Heine und das Judentum* [Heine and Judaism] (1867, publ. anonymously); *Virchow und die Juden* [Virchow and the Jews] (1868); *Der
   Sabbat in seiner kulturgeschichtlichen Bedeutung* [The significance of
   the Sabbath for the history of civilization] (1869, publ. 1881).

which had lain dormant since his Seminary days. Cohen countered Treitschke's intellectual condemnation or denigration of Judaism as "the national religion of a tribe that is alien to us" with a public declaration [3] in which he indignantly rejected what he considered to be a false interpretation of the distinctiveness of Judaism and hence of the Jew. He strongly affirmed his conviction that German Protestantism and liberal Judaism were not only equally enlightened but essentially alike. And venting his deep-seated and abiding abhorrence of any "nationalistic" interpretation of Judaism,[4] he suggested that the German Jew strive, in every way, for "the ideal of national assimilation." [5] Yet while he ardently expressed his love of the German ethos and whole-hearted identification with it, he also declared his unwavering belief in the supreme value of Judaism's basic concepts—its absolute monotheism, the pure spirituality of its God, and its Messianic and as yet unfulfilled but fulfillable hope and promise. He admonished his fellow Jews to deepen their understanding of and commitment to these concepts by serious study. And he made known, in no uncertain terms, his decision to take a stand at their side in the face of any threat to their religious convictions. In this sense, he had indeed "returned." From then on, he became increasingly concerned with and vocal about theoretical as well as practical Jewish problems; the detached philosopher changed into a devout (though not necessarily traditional) believer whose writings and lectures on Jewish subjects fill four substantial volumes.

At seventy, retiring from his position in Marburg, he moved to Berlin. There, he taught general and Jewish philosophy at the Academy for the Scientific Study of Judaism (*Lehranstalt fuer die Wissenschaft des Judentums*). The lectures he delivered there in 1913 and 1914 furnished the material for his most comprehensive

3. *Ein Bekenntnis zur Judenfrage* [A public declaration concerning the Jewish question].
4. As late as 1917, he wrote that "there is no Judaism except that of the Jewish religion" (*Neue Juedische Monatshefte*, 1917).
5. This assimilationist ideal did, however, not preclude his genuine appreciation of and sense of solidarity with Eastern European Jewry (see: "Closing of the Borders"). In fact, a 1914 educational mission to the Jewish population centers of Russia became one of the highlights of his professional and personal life.

and representative Jewish work, *Die Religion der Vernunft aus den Quellen des Judentums* (The Religion of Reason, Derived from the Sources of Judaism) which, though completed before his death in 1918, was published only a year later.[6]

The Religion of Reason is a multi-dimensional undertaking: it endeavors to give a systematic presentation of Judaism; it demonstrates the conviction of Cohen's later years that faith and reason need not be mutually exclusive; and it attempts to undergird Judaism philosophically, and to show that this religion of reason is not only intellectually respectable but also equal if not superior to much of the best in Western religious thought. Like Philo, Maimonides,[7] and Mendelssohn before him, Cohen seeks to synthesize two different cultures. To this end, he points out what to him seems an already existing German-Jewish spiritual symbiosis;[8] and he develops, subsequently, the thesis that the eternal verities of Judaism and the philosophical truths as defined by Kant and German humanism are all but identical.

Cohen's general philosophical orientation gave rise to his views on religion in general, and on Judaism in particular. He reiterated again and again that man's search for truth must be illuminated and guided by "scientific reason," or the "rationality of science," and that all science (as indeed all life) must be imbued with "reverence for truth." His own reverence for truth led him to develop what he called a "scientific philosophy," that is, a philosophy based on the all-inclusive principles of logic and reason. Emphasizing the supremacy of reason throughout his work, he sought to maintain the "historical character" of his system, for he

6. First edition, Leipzig 1919; a second edition, published in Frankfurt on the Main in 1929, was entitled *Religion der Vernunft aus den Quellen des Judentums,* omitting the article *Die.*

7. When Franz Rosenzweig, in a personal conversation with Cohen, commented on the similarity, in intent and impact, between *The Religion of Reason* and the *Guide of the Perplexed,* Cohen replied, with obvious pleasure, that he, too, felt his presentation would have satisfied the Rambam himself.

8. Cohen was the very epitome of a unique socio-historical phenomenon that flourished in the second half of the nineteenth and the first third of the twentieth century: the German-Jewish academic ("Herr Professor"), with the hyphen between German and Jewish not a symbol of mere punctuation but of an entire *Weltanschauung.*

felt that the continuity of "the history of scientific reason" must not be broken, since it reflects the progress of philosophy as such and therefore that of all culture. And philosophy as such meant idealism—an idealism "founded" by Plato and brought to full maturity by Kant.

Deeply steeped in the thought of both Plato and Kant, and lastingly influenced by what he saw as their "scientific" approach to man's crucial questions, Cohen evolved his own critical-idealistic theory: man cannot dispense with sense-experience, which provides his footing in the world of reality. But to make sense out of that experience and to evaluate the phenomena of this world, man needs his judgmental faculty, his reason. A critically interpreted reality, however, denotes more than the actually given. It represents not merely an empirical datum of the "is" but signifies an ideated dimension of the "ought."

The "ought" is the never-accomplished yet always-to-be-pursued task of ethics. Cohen sees ethics as an "eternal," that is, an ideal code of human action, valid forever and everywhere. Yet though not "concrete" in the existential meaning of the term, Cohen's ethics is by no means merely abstract, a principle operating in a vacuum. The good (as will be shown in a different context) is realizable, and in the here and now.

Ethics, therefore, must provide the motive power for man's every intellectual and spiritual endeavor. It is ethics alone which constitutes the true *raison d'être* of religion, and raises it from what Cohen regards as the murky depths of mythology to the enlightened heights of a *Kulturreligion* (civilized, or culturally advanced—and, by implication, exclusively Western—vs. primitive religion).[9] Mythology is irrational; it can do no more than indulge in idle fantasies about mankind's past, its "wherefrom," which determines man's fate. Looking backwards, mythology beclouds man's outlook and his understanding of life. But ethical religion is rational; it is purposefully concerned with mankind's future,[10] its

9. Not yet encumbered by the relativism with which contemporary sociology views societal "values," Cohen was quite certain of, and occasionally quite didactic about, the superior value of the absolutes in which he believed.
10. A future which Cohen is at pains to define as "historical," thus leaving

"where-to," which defines man's destiny. Looking ahead, religion gives direction to and sets goals for man's life.

This goal-orientation is one of the outstanding characteristics of Judaism, which, for Cohen, is the ethical religion par excellence. Ethics forms Judaism's very foundation, and informs all its goals and aspirations. Monotheism, prophetism, and Messianism are all manifestations of Judaism's "purposive ethics" and comprise its very essence.

But what, or who, serves as validation or as absolute criterion for Judaism's ethics and gives it "objective certainty" and constancy? Here, Cohen, the neo-Kantian, "hypothesizes" the idea of God. The term hypothesis as used by either Kant or Cohen does not suggest a tentative assumption, as it does in popular usage. Both philosophers define a hypothesis as a concept of fundamental significance, a notion so basic that all thought and all action are anchored in it. Hence, Cohen's hypothesis of the idea of God [11] in no way diminishes the grandeur traditionally associated with the religious concept of a personal God. For whereas, in Cohen's philosophy, the function of an idea is to establish criteria by which to judge the impressions man receives through his senses, the God-idea (though lacking the "concreteness" of a personal God) represents the foundation of all existence—its source, its goal-determinant, and its ultimate ethical criterion.

In his earlier works, Cohen had considered religion either as a handmaiden of ethics or as a transitional stage in mankind's moral development. Thus, he had tended to subsume religion under the general heading of ethics. But later, and particularly in his writings on Judaism, a new position emerges. True, he still draws no clear dividing line between ethics and religion. Although ethics determines man's relationship to man, and religion does the same for man's relationship to God, both derive their enduring significance

no doubt about its this-worldly character. Any definite notion of an other-worldly future, a "beyond," would have to be discredited as a mere myth.

11. A philosophically original but theologically vulnerable theory that has caused much debate among Jewish scholars.

from the idea of God; both are seen as manifestations of man's God-given reason.

With the idea of God thus underlying and overarching both ethics and religion, neither can be regarded as wholly independent of the other. Nevertheless, Cohen now ascribes to religion certain specific characteristics that do set it apart from ethics. These characteristics become evident in what he calls "correlation," a religio-philosophical term denoting the relationship that obtains especially between God and man but to some degree also between God and nature.

God's relationship to both man and nature is primarily that of creator to creature or creation. But this generative relationship, particularly with regard to nature, is augmented by a regenerative one in which God the Creator becomes manifest as God the Provider. That is, He continually "provides for" nature, renewing and sustaining it day by day, throughout the millennia and all eternity. Conversely, nature provides, by its continuous existence, the necessary physical setting or the material wherewithal for man's ever-to-be-renewed pursuit of an ethical life which will eventuate in the realization of the good on earth.

That realization of the good (a postulate of the divine-human correlation) is man's eternal task—eternal because both the goal and the God-idea are eternal. Striving to discharge this task of his, man relates himself to God. Nature and man are subject to change; God, however, is immutable, and in His immutability becomes the "guarantor" of ethics. God "guarantees" ethics in a twofold way: by the absoluteness of His being He vouchsafes for the absolute and infinite validity of ethics. And by having created man and endowed him with reason, He has also created the inherent warranty that man, though finite, can and will translate an abstract, ideal ethics into concrete, actual reality.

As Cohen speaks of God's being, of God the Guarantor, the Creator and Provider who maintains an ongoing relationship to nature and man, the philosopher's God-idea is made to coincide with Judaism's idea of God. In fact, Cohen now largely replaces the conceptual language of philosophy with the metaphorical language of religion, for he feels that both disclose the same or at least analogous insights. And he points with amazement to the Biblical Hebrew as that "primeval language" which, "emerging without any philosophical concepts, stammers the most profound word of any philosophy." [12]

That word is the name by which the God of Judaism is called, and which expresses His unsurpassed, unsurpassable majesty: *Yahveh,* which means "I am that I am," or, in Cohen's interpretation, "being as such."

God is, all-comprehensively, the One Who Is, and He is the Holy One. The concept of "holiness" is thus synonymous with the being of God, and corresponds to the concept of "morality" which is, or ought to be, synonymous with the being of man. When the Bible demands man's self-sanctification, asking that he become "holy," it does not mean that man should imitate God in an attempt—forever doomed to failure—to become "like" Him. It means that man should try to approximate God's holiness by living up to his own moral potential. For as he lives a moral life, man draws near to the holiness of God. This is the significance of the psalmist's verse: "The nearness of God is my good." [13]

God's holiness and man's morality are correlated, for "the principle of holiness, as applied to God, would seem to lack purpose if it were not also applied to and put into practice by man." [14] Cohen repudiates the "mystic delusion" that God's holiness constitutes a mysterious element of His nature.[15] Divine holiness—the eternal source of moral law—is not inaccessible to the cognitive faculty of man, and hence need not be revealed to him supra-rationally. Interpreting Isaiah's saying, "And God the Holy One is sanctified through righteousness" (Isaiah 5:16), Cohen holds that it is man's sanctification of God, or, in other words, his compliance with the moral law through righteous act or just deed, which "effects" God's holiness. In turn, it is God, and God alone, who effects man's

12. See "Uniqueness Rather Than Unity of God."
13. See "The Lyricism of the Psalms."
14. See "The Holy Spirit."
15. *Die Religion der Vernunft aus den Quellen des Judentums,* Leipzig 1919, pp. 128–129.

holiness (his sense of morality) by imbuing him with His own spirit.

For it is "the spirit of holiness," or the spirit of God, that comes alive in man through his act of self-sanctification. Holiness in man means neither sainthood—which belongs to the province of mysticism—nor an elated psychic state attainable through esoteric insights, nor even the performance of good deeds. To become holy is to come closer to the ethical ideal. To sanctify life is to impress upon it the mold of morality, to submit to an ethical code, to bring about, by one's every action, the realization of the good on all levels of personal and societal existence. Self-sanctification, or the awakening of God's holy spirit in man, means, then, that man, though aware of his own imperfection, takes upon himself the never-ending task to work for perfection—his own as well as the world's.

When Cohen refers to an awakening or unfolding of God's holy spirit in man, he therefore actually asks that man become conscious of his own rational faculty, his reason. For as spirit is God-given, so is reason.[16] Human reason, as the Creator's gift to His creature, has a spiritual dimension. Far from being merely a faculty of his theoretical intellect, reason "shapes as well as sustains" man's moral intellect, and thus becomes "responsible" for his moral action. And inasmuch as man's sense of morality is the correlate of God's spirit of holiness, reason becomes (as Ibn Ezra had stated earlier) the mediator between man and God.[17] It is in this sense only that the relationship of man to God, or of God to man, is ever mediated, and that the spirit of holiness is common to both God and man.

Yet though the spirit of holiness establishes a conceptual link between them, Judaism insists that God and man are and must forever remain distinct entities. In His unalterable distinctiveness or, as it has been called, His total otherness, the God of Judaism is a transcendent God. For only a truly transcendent God can be the Creator of nature and man, the Author of the good, and thus

16. See "Reason, the Hallmark of Divine Creation."
17. See "The German and the Jewish Ethos I."

the Guarantor of ethics. Conversely, man, to be truly human, must keep his own distinctiveness. A creature is by definition distinct from its creator. Thus, when the Bible says that man was created in the image of God, it actually emphasizes the difference between God and man and not their similarity—or so it seems to Cohen who, as a neo-Kantian, interprets the term "image" to mean "idea" rather than likeness. Thus understood, man is not "like" God; instead, "the idea of man is grounded in the idea of God." [18] Or, put differently, man as a creature of God cannot be like God. Yet man as man has been endowed by God with a soul, which "represents the element of the divine in man's body" [19] and enables him to understand the nature of the good and its challenge.

Pantheism [20] makes no such distinction between God and man, but sees the underlying principle of all existence as unity: God and nature, hence God and man who is but part of nature, are one. By its identification of God with nature, pantheism robs both of their specific significance, for it reduces morality to the level of physiology.[21] The pantheistic universe has no room for the God of morality or for an autonomous ethics; nor is its cosmic soul filled with that spirit of holiness which bestows worth on the individual soul by instilling it with a sense of moral purpose.

In contrast with the pantheistic principle of cosmic unity, Judaism has developed the all-important concept of divine uniqueness,[22] thereby establishing an indispensable distinction between God and man and, concomitantly, enhancing the special significance of both.

Cohen's juxtaposition and analysis of the concepts of unity and uniqueness serve to illustrate his conviction that monotheism is intellectually and morally superior to all other forms of religion. Monotheism is the result of man's profoundest and most enlightened religious thinking. Once he has outgrown the mythological

18. See "On the Aesthetic Value of Our Religious Education."
19. *Ibid.*
20. "Cohen's *bête noir*," as M.M. Kaplan puts it in *The Purpose and Meaning of Jewish Existence*, p. 87.
21. See "Religious Movements of Our Time."
22. See "Uniqueness Rather Than Unity of God."

stage of his development, man tries to comprehend the world's multifariousness by looking for the one behind the many; he seeks the one immutable principle by which to establish unity in the face of diversity, wholeness in the face of fragmentation, stability and meaning in the face of the ceaseless and seemingly senseless change of phenomena which constitute his experience. Monotheism calls this principle God. And Judaism—as the only "pure" or "absolute" monotheism—centers upon the idea of God as the One and Only, or the Uniquely One (*einzig*).

God's unique Oneness (*Einzigkeit*) is not a numerical concept; its meaning-content far exceeds that of unity. The pagan Xenophanes also "intuited unity" when he conceived of the one god Zeus over against "a heavenful of gods," an impressive intellectual achievement making him "the precursor of monotheism in Greek thought." [23] Jewish monotheism obliterates even the remotest notion of a plurality of gods, and rejects any trinitarian interpretation of the godhead. But its specific significance lies less in its emphasis on God's singleness than in its stress on God's singularity. When Judaism declares that God is One, it makes not merely a quantitative statement. It says that God is beyond compare, and that His being (*Sein*) is unique, hence different from any and all other modes of being or existence (*Dasein*). It says, moreover, that being is immaterial and disclosed to man by reason alone, while existence is materially determined and open to man's sense perception.[24]

Judaism does not, however, say that God's uniqueness precludes or negates all other modes of being. On the contrary, the very uniqueness of divine being (or being as such) makes it mandatory that nature and man be brought into existence. The concept of creation, Cohen holds, is essential to monotheistic thinking, for becoming must, conceptually, be derived from being. The Uniquely One God, "the God of transcendence," [25] must therefore be perceived as the Creator of the world; otherwise, being and becoming

23. *Ibid.*
24. *Die Religion der Vernunft*, p. 51.
25. See "Affinities Between the Philosophy of Kant and Judaism", also, "Religious Movements of Our Time."

would be identical, as they appear in the "absurd" pantheistic notion of a God co-equal with or immanent in the world. This notion represents an irrational solution of the ancient problem of being versus becoming. But Judaism, the monotheistic religion of reason, solves this problem rationally by regarding the existence of nature and man as "a conceptual consequence of God's uniqueness," and creation as "an essential corollary" or "a necessary attribute" of God.[26]

If the Biblical story of creation can be rendered in the vernacular of "scientific" philosophy, the account of the revelation at Sinai can also be interpreted rationally so as to become acceptable to the logician and compatible with his critical idealism. Cohen insists that neither creation nor revelation are inexplicable mysteries. Far from unfathomable, both notions are entirely intelligible.[27] As a logical concept, creation determines the relationship of being and becoming, while revelation is concerned with the problem of communication between God and man, between the originator of all morality and its executor. Revelation is a necessary instrument of divine-human correlation (and, as such, of a priori significance to religion): God relates Himself to man by imparting to him the spirit of holiness, the spirit of morality. And man relates himself to God by concretizing this spirit, that is, by carrying out the dictates of his "practical reason."

Since Judaism has always thought of God as the Uniquely One from whom all wisdom or moral discernment proceeds, it has to define the way in which this wisdom can be transmitted to man. Cohen regards it as characteristic of Judaism's rationality that this transmission of divine wisdom is referred to as the "giving" and not as the "revealing" of the Torah, and that Moses has lived on in the consciousness of the Jewish people as "our teacher" and not as "our revealer." [28] This, he feels, reflects the Jew's awareness that any and all transmission of spiritual values constitutes a teaching.

Admittedly, Exodus depicts one particular instance of teaching as an external event, described in physical terms: the revelation at

26. See "Uniqueness Rather Than Unity of God."
27. See "Reason, the Hallmark of Divine Creation."
28. See "Uniqueness Rather Than Unity."

Mount Sinai. But this Biblical account of the giving of the Torah should not be taken as Judaism's definitive statement on revelation; it should be understood, rather, as the beginning of a process of conceptual spiritualization which Cohen traces to Deuteronomy. There, "the word" is placed into man's own mouth and into his heart: the notion of the Torah's origin has become completely internalized. For Deuteronomy already realizes that "the teaching" (viz. ethical insights leading to the acceptance of a moral code) need not be revealed to man supranaturally. It must be brought to him neither from heaven nor from across the sea; it is a product of his own mind. Or, as Cohen puts it, "Revelation is the creation of reason." [29]

Man's mind or his reason, though, is not self-created. It has, as Cohen constantly reiterates, been put into man by God, the Creator of the spirit of holiness, which is merely a synonym for the spirit of morality. The assertion, therefore, that the Torah, "this holy moral law," "originated in man himself in no way contradicts the concept of divine revelation. In fact, to say that this law flowed from man's heart and mind is to say that it was revealed by God," for it was God who " 'formed the spirit of man within him' " (Zechariah 12:1).[30]

It seems evident that the Biblical accounts of creation and revelation—apart from any theological or philosophical significance—represent an attempt by early Judaism to throw light on the beginnings of the world and mankind. Yet Cohen sees Judaism's special distinctiveness not in its concern with mankind's past but in its hope for the future.

Hope, mankind, future—these three words appear and reappear in all of Cohen's Jewish writings; for him, they sound the keynote and comprise the message of prophetic Judaism. And for the founder of neo-Kantianism, prophetic Judaism is the "ideal," hence the only true and "real" Judaism. Prophetic Judaism, whose main component is Messianism, is the religion of hope, the religion of a united mankind, and thus the religion of the future.

29. *Die Religion der Vernunft*, p. 84.
30. See "Uniqueness Rather Than Unity."

The prophets "discovered" the concept of mankind and gave a new meaning to the concepts of "hope" and "future." Whereas other ancient peoples see their golden age in their past, and whereas mythology looks for a paradise lost, the Jewish prophets envision a Messianic age that will encompass all the nations of the earth. Prophetism thus gives shape to and indeed creates the future. The prophet's vision of "the end of days" is neither a euphoric dream nor an eschatological prediction. It is a teleological formulation of his hope that Judaism's ethical ideals of universal justice and universal peace will become historical reality.

The prophet's hope is not characterized by that shallow optimism which idly wastes the potential of the present by indulging in fantasies about a roseate future. It is rather a conscious forward thrust of the present into the future, a belief that the given can be transformed into or at least made to approximate the divinely demanded. Thus, it enhances all human existence with its confidence. Founded on the unshakeable trust that the future will keep its divine promise if man will only bend his every effort to effect a betterment of the present, the hope of the prophet, as "Messianic hope," represents and generates the Jew's solemn expectation that goodness and truth will in the end win out over evil and falsehood. Hope becomes faith, and the Messianic idea becomes the quintessence of the Jewish religion.

This idea is inseparable from the idea of mankind, which Cohen regards as "the highest triumph of religion." [31] Classical Greek philosophy could not conceive the idea of mankind because it had not conceived an idea of man. Even Plato lacked a comprehensive concept of man: his ideal man had to be a Greek (the foreigner was the barbarian) and a philosopher-king at that. And men in general, far from having been created equal, were to be divided into certain social classes and assigned certain tasks based on their social state at birth and their innate intellectual differences.

But prophetic Judaism could and did develop the idea of mankind because it had an idea of man. And it had an idea of man because it had an idea of God as the Uniquely One, the father of all men alike, who created man in His own image. God's fatherly

31. *Die Religion der Vernunft,* p. 280.

love, therefore, is not the exclusive birthright of the Jews; it is all-inclusive. "God loves the stranger" too.

This insight gives rise to the commandment "love your neighbor"—not "as yourself" but, as Cohen says, "because he is like you." For " 'reah' means the other, the one who is like you. He is the Thou of the I.[32] Prophetic Judaism is not content to have one man living alongside the other. It asks that each man live with and for the other and thus make of his fellow creature his fellow man. As fellow man relates himself to fellow man, their ethical interaction, characterized by empathy and compassionate love, will, Cohen suggests, lead to a dual disclosure: each will become aware of the other as his Thou, and thereby of himself as an I.[33] Moreover, as both recognize their common origin, they will recognize their common goal: as creatures of the One God, they must become the creators of the one mankind.[34]

Cohen sees in Judaism's concept of mankind "the archetypal, the fundamental Gestalt envisaged by moral man," "the principle of all that is human, in the individual, the state, and world history." [35] The postulate of one mankind as logical consequence of the idea of One God represents a unique cultural phenomenon. For while the ethics of philosophy is mainly concerned with the conduct of the individual, and therefore addressed to him, the prophet exhorts an entire people to live up to its God-given moral potential, that is, to fulfill its God-given ethical task. And inasmuch as Israel's task is to bring about the realization of the Messianic idea of universal justice, peace, and brotherhood, the prophet becomes the spokesman for a national ethics which points beyond itself and demands a supranational ethics.

Here, more than anywhere else, the teleological character of

---

32. See "Selfhood Through Ethical Action," an excerpt from a study of the Ethics of Maimonides, published in 1908, fifteen years before Buber's *I and Thou* appeared in print. There is, however, an important difference between Cohen's and Buber's concept of I and Thou: the former ascribes to it logical, the latter ontological significance.
33. *Die Religion der Vernunft,* pp. 22, 193, 209.
34. This interpretation of prophetic thinking is not unlike a concept Buber was to develop later: once man has learned to speak the "primary words" I and Thou, he must learn to say the "essential we."
35. See "The German and the Jewish Ethos I."

Messianism becomes evident, and prophetic vision becomes historical perspective. For the prophet teaches that the particular concerns of any one people, though legitimate in themselves, must eventually be superseded by the universal concerns of mankind. National history must become world history. With this new concept, the future is given an equally new dimension. It is no longer merely a temporal extension of the present, a time-to-come. As "Messianic" future, it is a conceptual expansion or ideal projection of today's "now" into tomorrow's "then," which, enlightened by a "new morality," represents Isaiah's "new heaven" (Isaiah 65:17). And this new heaven will reflect its light back upon the "new earth," which is a new reality, created by and representing a united mankind.

To make this prophetic vision come true is to understand the will of God, and to understand His will is to "know" Him. But knowledge of God means, to the prophet, moral awareness. Plato thought only a selected few capable of acquiring true (that is ethical) knowledge; Judaism, however, regards all men as inspirited by God and hence able to understand and carry out His moral mandate. Moreover, Judaism considers knowledge of God synonymous with love of God. And since love of God implies love of man, it also implies ethical conduct, which in turn becomes man's instrumentality for bringing about the "kingdom of God."

The kingdom of God is the ultimate goal of world history and its justification. And since it is not a celestial empire but a time when the ideal "ought" will become the actual "is," it cannot be brought about by a personal Messiah but only by the ethical practices of individuals and nations.

The kingdom of God represents a state of individual and societal redemption, a time when both man and mankind will have been delivered from spiritual enslavement. But redemption, too, cannot be achieved through the act of a personal Messiah. Indeed, Cohen refutes the rendition of the designation "Messiah" as "Christ." Though at one time Judaism did think of the Messiah in personal terms, placing its hope in one who would redeem Israel from her national misfortunes and restore her to national glory, it outgrew this early notion, replacing it with the "ethico-cultural concept of Messianism." [36] But even at an early stage of its development, Judaism never thought of the Messiah as the savior who would redeem the individual from his sins. For Judaism looks upon sin not as a manifestation or inescapable consequence of man's innately evil nature, but as a temporary transgression. And it looks upon man's transgression not as fateful evidence of ancestral guilt, but rather as his own digression from the right path, his own failure to stay on the mark set for him by the God of morality, "the Author and Guarantor of the Good." Man can therefore achieve redemption only through his own act of repentance, his own sincere, unmediated effort to "return" to the right path. Once he sets right the course of his life, however, and acts in accordance with moral law, man's inner sense of direction is restored and his reconciliation with God accomplished. [37]

Society at large can also be redeemed from its sins or ills only by its own efforts. Identifying himself completely with Judaism's ethico-cultural goals and aspirations, Cohen feels that universal justice, peace, and brotherhood represent a Messianic postulate rather than a Messianic promise. He therefore advocates man's tireless participation in the endeavors of all religious, cultural, civic or political institutions which can directly or indirectly contribute to their realization. Such participation will weld an aggregate of more or less isolated and often egocentric individuals into a purposefully interrelated community.

Cohen is firmly convinced that the modern state represents, at least potentially, such a community. As he conceives of it, the state is not a self-serving organization but an institution for the concretization of humanity's loftiest ideals. Rather than an end in itself, the state is a means to exert a moralizing influence on the individual. It must, at all times and under all circumstances, promote not only the general good of its citizens, but inculcate in them a sense of the good as such. Above all, however, the state is a means to fur-

36. See *Ibid.*
37. See "The Day of Atonement" and "The Concept of Reconciliation."

ther in its citizenry an understanding that "man's love for his own country is not invalidated by his cosmopolitan views," [38] and that universalism is not only compatible with real patriotism, but actually its necessary corollary. In this sense, and despite its intrinsic worth, the state is also self-transcending, for it ". . . culminates in the postulate of a federation of nations, and thus becomes the quintessence of ethics. The realization of morality on earth must consequently be brought about by the state as a symbol of a federation of nations." [39]

Cohen sees a federation of nations as the politico-organizational forerunner of a spiritually united, ethically motivated mankind. However, just as Messianism does not envision the disintegration of all nations but rather "their unification in a spirit of morality," so a federation of nations "would not mean the disappearance of different states but merely their alliance for the establishment of a genuinely international law." [40] By training the sights of its members on a mutually beneficial goal, such an alliance, Cohen hopes, would teach them to look beyond their countries' narrow self-interest, and thereby put an end to much of the antagonism that has habitually poisoned the atmosphere of international politics and spawned a seemingly endless succession of wars.

Once political thinking is guided by the idea of a united mankind,[41] a federation of nations will become the natural vehicle for the eventual elimination of war. Deeply rooted in prophetic Judaism, Cohen is a passionate advocate of peace,[42] repudiating the still extant belief of the ancient Greeks that war is the father of the world and its inevitable fate. Man is not only free but obligated to work for peace in every possible way. "War is the Satan of world history"; [43] but world history's very purpose is peace, and man is destined to achieve it. For Judaism—placing its faith not in a

38. See "Love of Religion."
39. See "A Reply to Dr. Martin Buber's Open Letter," written four years before the establishment, in 1920, of the League of Nations.
40. See "Religious Postulates."
41. Which, qua idea, always has reality even though as yet no actuality.
42. Though not an absolute pacifist, he felt that "a just war serves as preparation for perpetual peace" ("The German and the Jewish Ethos I").
43. See "Affinities Between the Philosophy of Kant and Judaism."

Messiah who already has come but in a Messianic age that must and surely will come—is confident that man will learn to prevent those Satanic incursions into his history so that he himself will bring healing to a racked and torn world.

Cohen's passion for peace and compassion for a suffering world lead him to align himself with the ideological goals of socialism. But his socialism, inspired by his religiously and philosophically grounded idealism, expresses itself in terms of pure ethics rather than practical politics. He sees society's shortcomings and the falseness of many of its values; and he particularly deplores the fact that the vast majority of men are still enslaved by a dehumanizing poverty. Declaring that society's status quo is not sacrosanct, he pleads for its change. He feels, however, that this change cannot be effected by social reforms alone; nor would it be the automatic result of any party politics. A change in man's social conditions must be motivated by an inner renewal of man's moral values.

Effecting this inner renewal is Judaism's as yet unaccomplished mission. And carrying the burden of this mission constitutes Israel's chosenness. The particularism intrinsic to the task, Cohen contends, is justified by the universalism of its goal and is, in a sense, self-liquidating. For Israel's chosenness is nothing but "history's means to accomplish the divine chosenness of mankind." [44] It is "the battlecry for divine justice" and places upon the Jew the "vocation to proclaim the One God as the redeemer of mankind." [45]

To carry out its mission, Israel must continue to live, as the prophet puts it, "like dew among the many nations," if only to symbolize by its physical dispersion its spiritual affirmation of the goals of universalism. In consonance with his evangelistic interpretation of Judaism, Cohen rejects the rationale of Zionism as well as its political efforts, refusing to acknowledge the need for the establishment of a "Jewish Homeland." Not only is the Jew factually at home wherever he is made to feel at home: but a Jewish homeland must be thought of in temporal rather than spatial terms if the Jew is to remain true to his religion and its Messianic postulate. Jerusalem, therefore, is significant not in a geo-political sense

44. See "Religion and Zionism."
45. See "The Style of the Prophets."

but as "a moral concept of the new world history"; and it is not Palestine but the Messianic age that beckons us as "our real Promised Land." [46] Israel is to "return" not to any particular topographical spot on earth but to God's "holy mountain," and not by itself, but as part of the one mankind that will acknowledge the One God. As bearer of a world-historical task, the Jew must see "the entire historical world as [his] future abode." [47] In short, Judaism's and Jewry's only true home is the future.

Cohen's repudiation of Zionism is, however, not due to his Messianic belief and his universalistic reading of history alone. To some extent, it is attributable also to his fervent German patriotism which leaves no room for any other "national" claim upon his loyalty. Cohen considers Germany not only as the political fatherland and cultural motherland of the indigenous German Jew but as the matrix from which a large segment of Western Jewry— including all those East European Jews whose mother tongue is Yiddish—has grown and received its spiritual values.

Those values—the creation of the German heart and mind, of Germany's famous "poets and thinkers"—are, Cohen contends, unmatched by anything any other modern nation has produced. The German Jew and his East European and overseas coreligionist need, therefore, look nowhere else for spiritual and cultural sustenance: Germany is not merely the most civilized country in the world but the hub of the cultural universe.

As the seat of all culture and learning, Germany is also the sanctum of religion,[48] guaranteeing not merely its free practice but promoting its scholarly, scientific study. In fact, Germany's ethico-cultural and intellectual atmosphere has contributed significantly to the progress of religion as such; strengthening the spiritual bonds between Protestantism and Judaism, it has been conducive to an unprecedented flowering of Jewish religious thought. In this sense, Germany has become the motherland of the Jew's soul, if his reli-

46. See "A Reply to Dr. Martin Buber's Open Letter."
47. *Ibid.*
48. That is, German Protestantism and liberal Judaism. Cohen ignores Catholicism almost completely, despite its numerical strength in Germany, and excludes from his deliberations all other religions and religious denominations.

gion be his soul.[49] Moreover, Cohen feels that the noble spirit and the lofty ideals which characterized the neohumanism of German philosophy and literature in the late eighteenth and early nineteenth centuries [50] are in such accord with the spirit and ideals of prophetic Judaism that the German Jew owes his country not merely a citizen's freely given allegiance but vastly more: a son's filial love.

Since the ethos of the German state is wholly congruent with that of prophetic Judaism, German nationalism and Jewish religiosity are mutually enhancing. But since the establishment of a Jewish state (as envisioned by Zionism before the end of World War I) represents no less than a denial of Judaism's mission, Jewish nationalism and Jewish religiosity are mutually exclusive. Given these premises, German nationalism is near-sacred and becomes instrumental to religious progress, whereas Jewish nationalism is near-sacrilegious and becomes detrimental to it. In fact, Jewish nationalism constitutes an ideological regression from cosmopolitan universalism to parochial particularism.

In keeping with his neo-Kantianism, Cohen once stated that all love—including love of God and physical love—is an idealization of its object.[51] Accordingly, love of country would necessarily imply its idealization. But does love of one's country also necessitate or justify its idolization?

This question, though obviously rhetorical, becomes more poignant from the vantage point of the more than fifty years of historical perspective of the cataclysmal experience since Cohen's death. Even if one were to disregard the tragically grotesque discrepancy between Cohen's image of Germany and that imposed by Hitler, it would still be evident that Cohen, the foremost proponent of critical idealism, all too often failed to judge reality critically though he invariably interpreted it ideally. Thus, this Jewish and socialist champion of human rights extolled Martin Luther as the liberator of man's religious consciousness but did not condemn him

49. See "The German and the Jewish Ethos I."
50. As exemplified, among others, by Kant's concept of perpetual peace and Schiller's ideal of universal freedom and brotherhood.
51. *Die Religion der Vernunft*, p. 187.

as the rabid Jew-hater he became in his later years, nor as the upholder of a social order that granted all privileges to the prince while denying them to the peasant. And by the same token, the philosopher could still effusively admire German high-mindedness and speak emotionally of Germany as the land of potential if not actual perfection at a time (1914) when most of the world had already become painfully aware of her serious national shortcomings and the threat of her military aggressiveness.

Nor was Cohen's religious posture entirely free of uncritical emotionalism,[52] a fact of which he himself was aware. In his personal approach to religious problems, he faced a predicament shared, in degrees, by anyone who is not an undeviating traditionalist: a conflict between his emotional religious needs and the strictly rational demands of his stern logic. He felt, however, that his logic usually won out in this struggle, as evidenced by an excerpt from a letter he wrote in 1917: "I have a fate of a peculiar sort. As you know, my heart and my feelings respond deeply to the emotional aspects of our religion; but abstraction is my fate." [53]

Abstraction was, of course, also the prime requisite if not one of the sancta of his profession; nevertheless, he was not always successful in his often stated resolve to keep his "instinctual attachment" to Judaism from interfering with his "scientific" method of investigating its theoretical religious problems. True, he never abandoned his belief in the hegemony of reason in all strata of human life. Yet in the sphere of personal commitment, he frequently, though incongruently, allowed his "heart and feelings" to color his religious thought, declaring simply: "The God of my heart is the God of my mind." [54]

52. He could, in fact, become quite sentimental about Judaism and Jews. He was, for example, particularly offended by Spinoza's rejection of Judaism's central ideas because it occurred in a period when Rembrandt, living in the same narrow alley, immortalized in his paintings the "ideality of the Jewish type." Similarly, he supported his ethico-cultural arguments for the admission of East European Jews to Germany by emphasizing their saintly looks which had impressed even a Gentile writer.
53. Quoted by S.H. Bergmann, *Faith and Reason*, transl. and ed. by Alfred Jospe, p. 41.
54. See "Love of Religion."

Writing on the significance of the Sabbath and other holy days, for example, Cohen repeatedly touches upon certain customs and ceremonies; but while he nostalgically and almost sentimentally evokes the mood of their observance, he strangely neglects to establish any criteria to justify that observance. The same holds true for the way in which he deals with the issue of prayer. Here, the stern logician does not even question the principle of prayer as such, that is, the possibility or impossibility of praying to a God whom he has elsewhere defined or hypothesized as pure idea, as a God of morality but without personality. Instead, his discussion of prayer (as exemplified by the Psalms) [55] reads like a personal confession of faith. In fact, the author's sensitive description of the psalmist's piety is genuinely moving because it conveys a sense of his own existential confirmation of the lyricist's religious stance.

Permitting himself to let his "soul speak," Cohen all but bears witness to the spiritual efficacy of prayer. Moreover, and rather startlingly, this "dialogical monologue" of man implicitly effects a fundamental transfiguration in Cohen's system: it transmutes the logical concept of God's and man's correlation into the psychological concept of an experienced divine-human relation.

Now, man's longing for and love of God are no longer interpreted as an intellectual search for moral truth alone. Expressed in prayer, it becomes a "genuine experience of the soul." And Cohen speaks feelingly of prayer as of that "psychological miracle" which reveals man's longing for a "unified heart"—that consummate state of saving grace in which all his moral contradictions and ethical conflicts are resolved. In this sense, prayer achieves man's redemption; it heals the rift in his doubt-ridden soul, restoring him to psychological and moral wholeness.

To accomplish that unity of heart and mind which symbolizes man's moral wholeness and intellectual integrity is Cohen's ultimate religious and philosophical concern. And it is this concern which motivates him to prove that religion and philosophy or, more specifically, prophetic Judaism and neoclassical idealism are but two different paths to the same goal. In fact, he does not al-

55. *Die Religion der Vernunft, Das Gebet* [On Prayer], pp. 438 ff. See also "The Concept of Reconciliation."

ways keep these paths or thought-systems separated, but often speaks of religion in the "scientific" idiom of philosophy. And since this cannot easily be accomplished without doing violence to either religion or philosophy, one occasionally gets the uncomfortable feeling that the philosopher applies to religion Procrustean rather than scientific methods in his effort to fit the Jewish God of his traditional cantor-father or of the Breslau Seminary into the mold of his neo-Kantian system.

On the whole, though, Cohen's attempt to rationalize religion and spiritualize philosophy by disclosing their common ground is eminently successful. His writings on Judaism constitute a landmark in the history of modern religious thought, and deserve a place in any series of Jewish classics.

Moreover, Cohen's compelling analysis is not only helpful but almost indispensable to any real understanding of Judaism's continued intellectual and spiritual significance. True, much of the *Zeitgeist* that fires his work with high-flown enthusiasm and on occasion breaks into overblown rhetoric is alien to the disillusioned, starkly realistic spirit of our own time. Obviously, what one age calls noble, another may call simplistic; and the ideal of one era may seem to be illusion or anachronism to another. Thus, Cohen's conviction that morality is indivisible [56] will be unacceptable to the adherents of situation ethics. His doctrine of Judaism's mission may seem untenable to those who seriously question the moral and theological implications of this concept. And his indomitable optimism and axiomatic belief in the basic goodness of man and the moral efficacy of education may appear naive to a generation made skeptical if not cynical by its own critical appraisal of recent and contemporary history.

Yet Cohen was no Pollyanna, and his optimism implies no blithe disregard of the so-called realities of life. His ideological orientation conveys not merely a sense of sanguine serenity but quite as much a sense of profound earnestness, with both his serenity and earnestness deriving from his trust in God and in man. For though he knows that man can and indeed all too often does "turn bad," he remains confident that even the evil-doer will

56. See "Uniqueness Rather Than Unity."

INTRODUCTION **39**

ultimately return to his original state—the good creature of a good Creator. Moreover, the critical idealist fully realizes that it takes man's best effort to transform the actually given into the ideally postulated; and he stresses again and again that the Messianic ideal lies on the near side of man's horizon.

This core meaning of Cohen's work has in no way been invalidated by the attitudinal divergence between the nineteenth and the twentieth centuries,[57] by the shift, for instance, from an essentially universalistic to an existentially particularistic world view. The Messianic ideal of one mankind under One God— whether interpreted in religious or philosophical terms—may have lost some currency today; and it may even appear sadly tarnished to the contemporary Jew. Yet it has not only retained its ultimate relevance for the Jew, but may actually help a world rent by an all-destructive divisiveness to regain its lost sense of humanity. And the enlightened rationalism Cohen seeks to promulgate remains a special desideratum in today's prevalent irrationality and subsequent transvaluation of all values.

Cohen was uniquely well equipped to distill "the truth" of Judaism from its literary sources, and test it against "the truth" of classical Greek and German philosophy. That some of the conclusions he drew from his neo-Kantian interpretation of this or that source are admittedly arguable is of tangential significance. What is of central importance and makes Cohen's writings enduringly relevant is the fact that he finds in Judaism that ultimate principle of truth which, correctly understood, does not hover unattainably above man but informs his entire personality and permeates the totality of his life. It is in this sense that religion and philosophy, faith and reason, are conjoined, that "truth is veracity of being." [58]

---

57. Though Cohen's religious work dates largely from the first eighteen years of this century, it bears the unmistakable imprint of nineteenth-century thinking.
58. See "The Style of the Prophets."

CHAPTER 1

Religion and
Comtemporary Culture

Editor's Note

The second half of the nineteenth century was a time when German Jewry eagerly availed itself of the ever-widening opportunity to acquire a secular education. But with the rising of the educational level and the accompanying process of acculturation went a decline in Jewish literacy and in religious commitment and observance.

Hermann Cohen, the German-Jewish intellectual par excellence, however, found it not only possible but—by an inner logic—necessary to assign to religion a legitimate place within contemporary culture. In contradistinction to the view dominant among the educated of his days, he saw in religion not a stultifying and intellectually retarding element but "that creative spirit of God which is at work in history as well as in the mind of man."

While science and philosophy are indispensable tools for the acquisition of cognitive knowledge, religion is essential for the acquisition of moral understanding. For religion, grounded in rationally substantiated insights, is a teaching about God; and the God of Judaism is the God of morality. To believe in the God of Judaism means, therefore, to believe in the centrality of ethics in man's life, and to affirm man's membership in the moral universe.

But the Jew can arrive at such a belief and affirmation only when he knows and understands his religious heritage. Hence, religious education is of singular importance—for today's Jew quite as much as for tomorrow's Judaism.

Religious Postulates

It should be obvious to any educated person that only philosophy can devise—because it alone can substantiate—a *Weltanschauung*. And the recent claim by some spokesmen of re'igion that religion *as* religion can offer a world view is due precisely to that erroneous assumption which will be the main point of my discussion.

Religion considers itself to be, essentially, a teaching about God. And it also feels, and justifiably so, that there ought to be no positive *Weltanschauung* without a concept of God. But it makes a mistake when it assumes to be adequately equipped to substantiate and guarantee the idea of God. This popular misconception has, in fact, been refuted by the history of all religions. For in all of them, dogmatics—or the system of their religious tenets—emerges out of, and as, philosophy. Hence, there must be a natural connection between religion and philosophy. Religion, actually, can arrive at a reasoned theological position or, as it were, at the God of *Weltanschauung* only by virtue of such a connection.

Recently, however, the aversion against religion has become more pronounced among the educated, owing to their distrust of philosophy and lack of respect for it. Modern academicians view philosophy and religion with equal coolness, particularly with regard to the problem of God. This goes so far that a philosopher's scientific credentials are already suspect if he does not observe an official silence concerning theological questions.

This attitude, by now almost predominant in our circles, also constitutes the greatest threat and danger to our existence. For our existence is grounded in our religion, whose sole foundation is the idea of the One God.

Before going on, I must remind you that for decades we have neglected this fundamental idea in our religious discussions. We prefer to talk exclusively of our moral teachings because they seem to provide legitimate proof that we are decent people. But decent morals do not, by any means, constitute sufficient grounds on which to base a religion. A religion's right to exist is derived from its concept of God. And this concept must be constantly reaffirmed and perfected.

This is particularly true of Judaism which, as a matter of principle, makes no distinction between religion and ethics. For the God of Judaism is the God of morality. That means that His significance lies wholly in His disclosure as well as His guarantee of ethics. He is the Author and the Guarantor of the moral universe. This significance of God as the ground of the moral universe is the meaning of the fundamental principle of God's unity.

But what, actually, is the supreme distinction of this divine unity? The tasks posed by the moral universe are, after all, so manifold that one can understand why polytheism felt moved to distribute them among different gods. And how could one retain within Christianity the concept of one [1] God, even though in the form of a trinity?

The supreme distinction of God's unique Oneness does not consist in the difference between unity and plurality. Divine Oneness implies, instead, that difference between God's being and all being capable of being enumerated, which constitutes the true spirituality of our One God. Anything pertaining to the senses, and therefore also to anything human, is far removed from this God-concept, which, to us, implies the eternal, unshakeable, irreplaceable, primeval ground of the moral universe. Without this God-concept, morality might seem to us to be no more than the expression of a natural human inclination, and as such it could easily be a sweet delusion. . . .

This, then, is my first postulate: in our scholarly as well as in our popular treatment of religious questions, we ought to make the idea of God a guiding principle whose inexhaustible meaning we must come to comprehend ever more clearly.

1. "One," lower case, stands for a numerical concept, while "One," upper case, will be used throughout the text to convey a qualitative concept, as in the German "einzig"—one and only, singular, unique. E.J.

[In keeping with the spirit of our times, many Jews say:] Judaism, like any other religion, represents God's teachings; but we have no relationship to God. . . . These Jews cling to the predominant notion that universal education and full participation in European culture preclude a positive relationship to Judaism. . . . In the face of this idolization of universal education (and, unfortunately, also of specialized, scientific education) we assert: there can be no universal education, nor can there be any European culture or any ethics without the idea of the One God as the God of morality. For no culture has any ground or foundation without a scientifically reasoned ethics. But such an ethics, in turn, must be grounded in the idea of the One God. It can do without other gods but not without the One God. Consequently, there is neither a European culture nor an ethics in which Judaism does not have a fundamental share. . . .

Nature and morality are not one and the same, yet both have their origin in, and are vouchsafed by, the unity of God. But though nature and morality are and must remain different, they interact and are conjoined at a certain point: in man. For when I live in accordance with moral concepts, I am no animal, no mere creature of nature, but a member of the moral universe. It is, however, only the idea of God which gives me the confidence that morality will become reality on earth. And because I cannot live without this confidence, I cannot live without God. . . .

As my second postulate, I should like to discuss our relationship to the state. Like all questions pertaining to Judaism, this one too must be determined in the light of the concept of the One God. Because the One God is the God of morality, He exists primarily not for the individual, the family, tribe or nation, but for all mankind. Concern with the needs of the individual or the tribe is not lacking even in polytheism. Through its ancestral cult and graveside symbolism, mythical religion provides for the individual's and the tribe's continued existence in the beyond, and often also for atonement and absolution.

What is new and unique about the One God as the God of morality is the fact that He takes care not merely of the individual person or the individual people, nor even merely of the people among whom He first revealed Himself, but that He calls all nations to Himself; that He unites them all in the bond of one mankind, under the name of the One God who is the Father of all men; and that He holds out to them the promise of a time when a sense of ethics will be highly developed among all men. This in fact will be the infallible and only certain mark of their union under Him. Thus, and from the beginning, the One God implies a mankind united in the ideal of morality.

It seems we have gradually stopped talking of the national God of the Jews, or at least we do so only with a certain hesitation. But we are as yet far from drawing the right conclusions from the insight we have finally gained. I must limit myself here to a discussion of only those conclusions which have a bearing upon our relationship to the state.

Inasumch as the One God is the God of all mankind, He cannot be the God of only one nation. No matter how limited one's notions of the Messiah—who represents an age, the so-called "days of the Messiah"—one cannot possibly deny that the Messiah for Israel must also be the Messiah for all nations. Along with the Jews, therefore, all nations, even those from the remotest isles, must draw near to Jerusalem. Nor must there remain any distinction between the children of Israel and the sons of strange lands. For the latter, too, will some day become priests and Levites. Ahead of us lies an era in which the "new covenant" will be made, an age of which it is said, "I will put my law in their inward parts, and in their heart will I write it" (Jeremiah 31:33).[2] Ahead of us, that is, lies an era when all nations will say: "For Thou art our Father; for Abraham knoweth us not" (Isaiah 63:16). This is the way Jeremiah and Isaiah expressed their patriotism.

We should not, therefore, let anything keep us from adopting the profound political wisdom of the jeremiads as our guiding principle: "Weep ye not for the dead, neither bemoan him; but weep sore for him that goeth away, for he shall return no more, nor see

2. All Biblical passages will be quoted in the translation of the Jewish Publication Society of America, Philadelphia 1955, unless otherwise stated. See preface, p. 12.

his native country" (Jeremiah 22:10). This explains the tragedy of our wandering among the nations of the earth. The One God has taken our country from us so that He might give us the concept of mankind. The One God cannot be the God of any one country or state. He can be the God only of a mankind that is united in morality. It is therefore incumbent upon us to gain recognition in the world for this One God. This is our world-historical task.

Were it not or were it no longer for this mission of ours, the preservation of our community would have no specifically Jewish significance. Only this task of ours—the dissemination and deepening of the idea of the One God, and its elaboration throughout the millennia—only this mission on earth justifies and explains our continued existence as the creedal community of the One God.

Contemporary terminology should, therefore, no longer refer to a Jewish nation; for modern history and political science regard the nation merely as vehicle for the state. For this reason a distinction must be made between nation and nationality. The modern state requires a uniform nation but by no means a uniform nationality. Nationalistic movements are therefore wrong on theoretical as well as moral grounds not to take this distinction into consideration. . . .

Our way has been clearly marked for us by our history. And our history is but a manifestation of the essence of our religion. Just as the banishment from Paradise constitutes man's entrance into civilization, so does our banishment from our country usher in our global pursuit of the idea of the One God. As it is said: "And the remnant of Jacob shall be in the midst of many peoples, As dew from the Lord" (Micah 5:6). The establishment of a state of our own is incompatible with the Messianic concept and with Israel's mission.

Moreover, despite all the suffering and insults we have to endure as the destiny imposed upon us by our faith, or as the yoke of the kingdom of God, our dispersion has long ceased to mean exile to us. We do live in our native land, and we live in our state as well as for it. And it is this state of ours which makes available to us the blessings of general culture.

It is not true that we maintain, or even wish to maintain, a separate Jewish culture. The distinctiveness of Jewish culture is limited to its ethical concept of God, a concept it has contributed to general culture. But just as our great men have always derived their knowledge of mathematics, philosophy, and medicine, or the art of poetry from general culture, so do we ourselves participate fully in all these aspects of cultural life. It is in the domain of religion alone that we wish to preserve our distinctiveness. Here we are and intend to remain Jews. . . .

The task of teaching and indeed of living the idea of the true—that is, the truly One—God among the nations of the earth must continue to fill us with a sense of elation. But it is inherent in this task that we become an integral part of these nations and their cultural pursuits. Let their people be our people, for their state is our state [as their country is our country]. Except for our idea of the One God, there is nothing that sets us apart. We certainly do not pursue science and art or economic and civic matters in any specific way. In all these areas, we work in conformity with the methods and toward the goals of general culture. And cherishing these goals, we extend the love our country has instilled in us to its intellectual and moral concerns as well.

Love of our country is a necessary corollary of the idea of the Messianic God, as is our striving for a fatherland where we can be at home and where general culture and intellectual pursuits can flourish. For Messianic mankind by no means implies a disintegration of all nations, but rather their unification in a spirit of morality. Even a league of nations would not mean the disappearance of different states but merely their alliance for the establishment of a genuinely international law. The Messianic God does not represent merely a future image of world history, however. He demands—by virtue of the eternal ideas conjoined in Him—political action [in the present] and continuous, tireless participation in various concrete national tasks. It is the duty of any Jew to help bring about the Messianic age by involving himself in the national life of his country.

Every nation and every state has its world-historic task with regard to the actualization of the Messianic ideal. And in each state the Jew, too, must therefore selflessly and unreservedly pledge himself to the fulfillment of these national tasks, and bring to them all his energy and the full strength of his freely offered and pure love. Our state [that is, the country in which we live] is our fatherland. And it is our Messianic religion which, by its very nature, not only commands but also enables us to acknowledge and love our state as our fatherland. . . .

And as a third postulate, I am asking for a deepened concern with Jewish scholarship. . . . That we have had to take a back seat in Bible scholarship is clearly due to the fact that our scholars depend, outwardly as well as inwardly, on their congregations. Yet we ought to regain prominence in this—our very own—field. Even though we owe much of our understanding of prophetism to Protestant thought as taught at our universities, there too the influence of theology remains all too evident. Consequently, the Protestant concept of Messianism, circumscribed as it is by Christology, has not yet emerged with that profundity and clarity of the God-idea which we have developed naturally.

But if we wish to work once again effectively in the field of Bible scholarship, in a free scientific spirit as well as in accordance with the spirit of Judaism, we must gradually leave our literary ghetto—as Zunz has called it—and try to make our way to the university. For this is the forum where opposing views must be argued and reconciled. Of course, it will take some time before the walls of this intellectual ghetto of ours will fall. But it is beyond doubt that they will come down, as must all barriers to intellectual freedom among men, especially those among citizens of the same country. Until such time, though, we must remain and indeed become ever more intent upon deepening, broadening, and making more comprehensive the scope of our own teaching institutions so that their spirit will be commensurate with that of the university. Towards that end, we must vigorously and eagerly support the efforts which have recently been made regarding the promotion of higher learning among us. And this includes politics and science as much as religion.

In the last analysis, our political equality rests on whatever spiritual strength we can derive from our religious sources. Even from a purely political point of view we therefore urgently need an ever-increasing awareness that we as Jews derive sustenance and guidance not only from the modern culture that surrounds us but also from our specific Jewish culture.

But the duty to promote higher Jewish learning must also be seen as the most proper concern of religion. No religion can survive meaningfully in our contemporary culture if it persists in merely observing its customs, no matter how devoutly. All cultural life, including the religious, must involve the mind as much as the heart. It is not enough that our soul be satisfied with and exalted by our old customs and ancient spiritual treasures. These treasures must be acquired ever anew. They must be rediscovered by new efforts, and comparative studies must throw new light on them so as to give them creatively new forms. This holds true for Rabbinic no less than Biblical literature. And there is a rich, open field of which general scholarship is as yet totally unaware: the broad area of our religio-philosophical literature, which dates back to the ninth century.

Thus, this third task must be added to the first two. For only if we can demonstrate that throughout the history of our philosophy of religion—which is the history of our dogmatics—the interrelatedness of the ideas of the One God and of moral mankind has been acknowledged and affirmed, can we be convinced of the truth of our religion, and continue to profess it in all its majesty.

Love of Religion

Love of God implies love of religion. The commandment to love God is immediately followed by the injunction: "And these words, which I command thee this day, shall be upon thy heart; and thou shalt teach them diligently unto thy children . . ." (Deuteronomy 6:6–7). Our sages were aware of the connection between love of

God and love of Torah. Hence, it became a basic tenet of Judaism that love of God means knowledge of God: not knowledge of His essence but of His attributes. And God's attributes are the very epitome of what human morality should be; or, simply, they are the archetypes of human morality (Exodus 34:6–7). To love God is therefore to comprehend morality.[1]

But love and knowledge are not wholly equivalent. Moreover, may love, a human affect, really dare reach out to God, whom one obviously cannot "love" in the usual sense suggested by this term? Or is love more than a mere affect?

Love of God implies love of religion. And religion exemplifies that creative spirit of God which is at work in history as well as in the mind of man. Thus, one ought to love any religion, that is, religion as such, and in any form—as a manifestation of the moral spirit, the divine spirit of mankind. And learning and education will contribute to our sympathetic understanding of all civilized religions by widening our horizons. In fact, man's readiness to appreciate another's religion is the surest sign of his own genuinely religious and humanistic orientation.

But religions, like all other cultural phenomena, undergo many and multifarious changes. In this universal development, both nations and individuals will, at any given time, occupy different stages in their own relationship to religion. Any civilized man has his own religion, however, which has become his partly owing to his personal development, and partly because of certain social factors; hence, he cannot ever completely sever himself from it. True, he may deny or even leave this religion, at least to all outward appearances. But it will remain a component, no matter how latent, of his psychological and intellectual make-up.

It is a natural psychological process that turns love of religion as such into love of one's own particular religion. But is this kind of love justified? Not only is it justified—it is a natural duty of civilized man, provided it does not interfere with his universalistic, humanistic orientation. In fact, just as man's love for his own country must not be interpreted as detrimental to his cosmopolitan views, so his love for his own religion must not be mistaken for or condemned as zealotry or conceit. . . .

1. See "The Social Ideal," p. 67, ff.

Love of religion as such means, primarily, knowledge. Hence, love of one's own religion must also be grounded in knowledge. Moreover, our love for our Jewish religion is based upon our belief in its profound cultural significance and its distinct cultural value. As modern and civilized men, we could not cherish our own religion were we not unshakeably and utterly convinced that it is fully consonant with the ideals of modern culture. We know that our fundamental religous principles constitute the deepest roots of contemporary ethics, roots which have not withered and must not be permitted to wither if civilization's spiritual progress is to continue in an unbroken line.

Our love does not make us blind, however. We do not underestimate the contribution Christianity, and especially Protestantism, has made to the development of our civilization. We not only are aware of the link that once existed between early Christianity and Judaism—we keenly feel the need for establishing still closer ties between today's Christianity and Judaism, ties we must strengthen for our mutual benefit.

Our reading of history convinces us of Judaism's undying value for mankind's moral and cultural development. Love of our religion means, therefore, our full appreciation of our historical vocation and an affirmation not only of our past but of our present and our future right to exist.

When a religion is denied the right to its historical existence, its adherents are denied all historical honor, and thereby also their personal honor as believers. By cherishing our religion, we cherish our historical honor or the honor of our historical personality.

We do not think of ourselves as disturbing the religious harmony of our country, nor are we obstinate guardians of a blind alley of history. Thus, we seek no hollow, fictitious, false accord with those around us, an accord that would lack all real consonance because we would be out of tune with our own soul. We believe, instead, that we still have to sound a basic note in the harmony struck by the manifold ethico-cultural chords of the world.

We love the uniquely One God of our religion who remains for us, now as ever, wholly distinct from the God of the Trinity. Our uniquely One God is the profound, eternal idea that forms the basis of our religion. He is our "wisdom and understanding" (Deuteronomy 4:6) of which we shall never let go. Nor shall we let ourselves be dissuaded from holding fast to this wisdom and understanding by any of those pretenders to greatness who abound in our confused modern culture. . . .

In faithfulness we remember our teachers. We think particularly of the inestimable service rendered to Judaism by Abraham Geiger,[2] who, through his important scholarly research, established the religious centrality of our belief in our historical vocation. Our ancient sages were right: love is knowledge. Which means that no affect, not even the affect of love, suffices to give substance to our convictions. Historical honor, for instance, is a lofty concept; yet to be really substantiated, it must be derived from the clear, inexhaustible source of scholarly knowledge, or at least from an insight into the abiding value of our religious literature.

Though piety is a strong force, it alone cannot counteract the manifold inroads made upon our faith by our complex modern culture. It is not enough to love God as the "God of our fathers." He will be and remain "an everlasting rock" (Isaiah 26:4) only when He becomes "the rock of my heart" (Psalms 73:26). And only as the rock of my heart will He be "the rock of my salvation" (Psalms 89:27). The God of my heart is the God of my mind. The God of my salvation is the God of my religion.

My love must be undergirded and confirmed by knowledge. Love of our religion, therefore, means love of our writings, of the entire body of literature which has been instrumental in Judaism's spiritual development throughout history.

The cultivation of our religion must not be limited to public worship services. Our ancestors never conceived of nor meant to maintain their religion in so one-sided a manner. In fact, their constant and diligent pursuit of Jewish scholarship enhanced their aptitude not only for all learning but also for the arts or any other cultural activity as soon as they were given any access at all to those areas.

The assertion that our efforts to reach and maintain a high level

2. Abraham Geiger (1810–1874); foremost representative of Reform Judaism in Germany.

of cultural maturity leave us no time for the serious study of Judaism reflects a sad prejudice which fits in with the general pedagogical prejudice of our time. Moreover, it is our contention that those among us whose work represents a not inconsiderable contribution to the different cultural endeavors of our time draw on some inherited mental faculty that has been sharpened by millennia of religious learning.

Neither political nor social oppression nor even apostasy can do us as much harm as does the fact that our intellectual energy is no longer spent on any research into, or serious occupation with, our religious sources. No pride in our history and no love of our own people are a substitute for that strength which flows from the knowledge of our religious sources and enables us to give living testimony to our faith. Without knowledge of our literature we cannot arrive at a genuine religious conviction. And without a conviction of the cultural relevance of our religion, our love for our faith cannot endure.

Not all Jews need to become scholars. This prime requisite of ancient Judaism can probably no longer be upheld. But the modern world makes a distinction between education and scholarship. The educated Jew represents the link between those engaged in scholarly research and those active in commercial enterprises. To become religiously literate is the cultural task of all Jews; our religious literature must, therefore, become their common property. . . .

Our religion is *our* religion, constituting our privilege as well as our honor. To the degree that men may speak at all of possessing a divine truth, we can fully answer for the truth of our religion. We vouch, with our whole being, for its cultural significance—a significance that reflects not some past glory but an everlasting, an elemental force. Thus, our love of our religion charges us with the historical and politico-cultural task to preserve Judaism and maintain its relevance for the culture and ethics of mankind.

We can perform this task, however, only to the extent to which we become proficient in religious studies and religious learning. We do not wish to be praised condescendingly for our intelligence or virtuosity in any other field; we wish to gain recognition for our work on behalf of the truth of our One and Only God. The sermon preached in the fields of Moab moves us today even as it inspired our ancestors: "For what great nation is there, that hath God so nigh unto them, as the Lord our God?" (Deuteronomy 4:7). This "nearness" of God implies to us His absolute spirituality. "Take ye therefore good heed unto yourselves—for ye saw no manner of form on the day that the Lord spoke unto you in Horeb out of the midst of fire—" (Deuteronomy 4:15).

Our God's spirituality, admitting of neither form nor image, is the primal cause of His truth. To be congruent with this spirituality, our love of Judaism must be kept alive as knowledge, as study, and as learning. And we must bend every effort and make use of all cultural means at our disposal to demonstrate this love of ours in all its profundity and to represent it in all its purity.

On Jewish Education

Religious education must become a surrogate for religious scholarship, though substantively it cannot take its place. Every modern Jew ought to feel obligated to promote the scientific study of Judaism (Wissenschaft des Judentums). He must take upon himself the responsibility for its support and continuation, and with it the duty of personal study. Concern for the life of the synagogue or other religious institutions is not enough, for such endeavors must remain inadequate as long as the pressing need for the scientific study of Judaism is overlooked. No religion within modern culture can maintain itself by its cult alone. It will remain viable and creative, hence have a claim to continued existence, only through the pursuit of scholarship. The science of religion constitutes the best protection and defense of religion, for a scientific study of religious history renews and confirms the core-meaning of religious truth. Without an in-depth understanding of its past—with its resultant claim for the future—any modern religion lacks true significance and real life, no matter how firm its anchorage in or how strict its observance of rigid customs.

The Transcendent God: Archetype of Morality

The educated layman rejects the concept of God mainly because he takes exception to the notion of divine transcendence. This notion seems to him even more objectionable than that of an immanent divine personality which he might possibly find acceptable. But what actually is meant by transcendence?

It is a common assumption that this concept came into being and was universally established through revelation. It originated, however, in philosophy, and pagan philosophy at that. It was devised by Plato, though not specifically with regard to God but rather with regard to one of the Platonic ideas. It refers to the highest idea in which Plato's system of ideas culminates: the idea of the good. An idea, notion, or fundamental cognitive principle is defined as transcending all physical being. This transcendent mode of being cannot denote sensate existence because this would be incongruent with the concept "idea." It denotes its distinctiveness from nature's mode of being. The idea of the good represents as well as guarantees a mode of being that differs from nature's being —which is verifiable by mathematics. Transcending any mode of being verifiable by natural science, the idea of the good constitutes and substantiates the being of ethics.

Our prophets were no philosophers; but the spirituality of God had to be their guiding principle if they wished to establish the concept of unity as genuinely distinct from that of plurality. And what the prophet calls "spirit" evolved from the kind of intellectual orientation that led the philosopher to speak of "idea." That aspect of being which the prophet tries to distinguish from any physical form is, in the terminology of the philosopher, called transcendence.

Transcendence, then, denotes that mode of being which is not beyond all existence as such but beyond an existence verifiable by natural science. And where the philosopher refers to the idea of the good as "highest knowledge," namely ethics, the prophet speaks, in the same sense, of the One and Only God as the Holy One, namely the God of morality. The same tendency is expressed in our tradition's basic precept that we can know God's essence only through His thirteen attributes, which are moral attributes; and that, hence, we can conceive of Him only as we conceive of the idea of the good.

This is the simple, profound, true meaning of God's transcendence. God is in truth "beyond me," for He is the Holy One, the archetype of all human morality. This archetype serves not merely as an exemplar; rather, it represents the ground of all law, and is as such the basis for both morality and natural science. Only when one denies moral law can one deny God. But once one accepts the existence of a natural law one cannot be a skeptic concerning moral law.

But could it possibly be said that pantheism offers a substitute for God, that is, for God as the archetypal law of morality? Rather than offer a substitute for this God-concept, pantheism implies its nullification, for it makes the basic methodological mistake of obliterating all qualitative differences between nature and ethics.[1] Kant was therefore right in his rejection and criticism of Spinoza, the scholastic. The superficial mind of the half-educated has always been impressed by Spinoza's high-flown statement that he would "define" human actions and passions as if he were treating of geometrical lines and planes. Kant, in contradistinction, says that as far as a circle is concerned, I should not ask what it ought to be but study its properties instead. As far as human volition is concerned, however, I may and indeed must ask: what should man will?

Anyone who considers monism a scientific, methodologically

1. See "The Holy Spirit."

substantiated truth is a pantheist who not only has no God but who also has no distinctive ethics. And just as Kepler still harbored the superstition that all celestial bodies were endowed with a soul because of their ability to execute with such precision the laws he had discovered, so do modern biologists still harbor the scientific superstition that there is no qualitative difference between an ethics ideated by the human mind and that mode of being which is manifest throughout the physical world. Yet to criticize pantheism as atheism misses the mark. It would be more correct to define it as amorality, for it actually cancels out morality by reducing it to the level of physiology.

Yet it must not be assumed that the controversy about God is, strictly speaking, merely a methodological dispute about the concept or modes of scientifically verifiable being. This assumption becomes untenable as soon as one considers the fundamental significance of the God-idea.

What is the inner connection between belief in God and the very foundations of the moral universe? To put the question this way is to reverse the issue. When the monists deny God or any distinction between nature and morality, one could indeed call this a methodological problem which at most concerns man's anthropological nature—whether he be more or less, cat or dog. But what is of real import to mankind and its history is beyond the ken of this controversy. True, ants and bees do live in organized societies. Yet these can hardly be totally equated with the societal structures evident throughout world history. Nor can one say that a beehive represents the aesthetic principles of architecture, though it may indeed be built according to its mathematical principles. Moreover, even if I were but an animal, I would still not give up my theoretical interest in the state systems as they were developed throughout world history. The question, therefore, remains: what is the goal of mankind's political history? But to ask this question is equivalent to inquiring into man's ethics.

Does it really make sense, scientifically or methodologically, to speak of man's actions as one would of geometrical lines, when these actions set the world stage for and affect the politics and world history of mankind? And is it really proper for a biological methodologist to say that nature and morality are identical? Can these two actually be explored experimentally, and by the same methods? And can one possibly still hold on to the popular preconceived notion that by studying nature one necessarily studies morality too?

This brings us, once again and quite unintentionally, to the connection between the concepts of God and of the Messiah. God does not merely provide us with the ground rules by which to control our passions. He is the archetype of morality, as revealed to historical man. And by this is meant not a model for man, much less an image of man, but rather the archetypal law of morality. For our concept of man can be fully realized only by a united mankind, with all nations and states as vehicles for man's advance toward this goal.

A united mankind, then, is what ethics is really about. This is the only way to "define" the problem, if such a definition is meant to establish an analogy between ethical and mathematical problems.

And here arises the question: through what ideas, and on what premises and principles can I achieve the solution of this problem, the realization of this goal? For ethics remains a set of theories as long as I do not translate its moral postulates into practice.

At this point, our concern is no longer with transcendence. We needed this concept to outline the problem. But with the solution of the problem [that is, work for a unified mankind] goes the dissolution of the concept [of transcendence]. For reality will always mean realization; rather than coinciding with some given actuality, it hovers over the realm of action. And this realm of moral action must be conquered and maintained ever anew. In no way can man's actions therefore be considered as analogous to geometrical lines or motions of physical points, as the original methodology of pantheism would have it. They are, rather, motivated by moral considerations, and thus become instrumental in establishing that moral universe for which individual nations can strive through a confederation of their states.

This confederated mankind represents man's Messianic future. And we who profess Messianic monotheism believe in this Messianic mankind. The Messianic God is mankind's redeemer and, through mankind, the redeemer of man. The concept of a united mankind represents the apex of man's moral awareness; and it is only the crest which determines the full extent of the foundation. In the transcendent God we recognize the God of that morality which is distinct from all natural forces: the God of world history and as such the God of mankind. Because of our historico-political beliefs, and in contradistinction to the biological metaphysics of monism, we hold fast to the God of history.

Therefore we must regard pantheism as philosophically immature. God is distinct not from the world but from nature. The term "world" implies history, while the term "nature" comprises everything from planets to single cells. To us, "world" has come to mean world history. History has extended man's scientific horizon beyond the laws of nature. It is this scientific approach, this philosophical belief (which is methodologically related to science) that takes us beyond the preliminary philosophical stages represented by pantheism and makes us adherents of Messianic monotheism.

Because of this orientation of ours, we feel reassured about Judaism's future. We are confident that the continuous scientific progress of our time will create a climate in which conceptual thinking will gradually replace slogans appealing to superficial and fickle minds; and that it will induce an attitude of reasoned judgments dictated by the heart and nurtured by a piety rooted in historical awareness. We are confident, too, that it will be possible to restrain those alarming elemental forces which manifest themselves in the hostilities and conflicts of nations and impede their progress toward mankind's goal.

No one who is able to observe the cultural scene from a scientifically oriented philosophical vantage point can doubt the correctness and veracity of our views. But the fact that we need not fear for the future does not free us in any way from our present obligations. No politico-ethical individual must ever think that the task of the present may be safely left to the future.

CHAPTER 2

Classical Idealism
and the Hebrew Prophets

Editor's Note

Cohen sees an inner affinity between Greek philosophy, as exemplified by Plato's classical idealism, and Jewish religion, as exemplified by its "classical" proponents, the Hebrew prophets. Both Plato and the prophets see the ideal behind the real: the world of the senses is not the seat of all truth. Human existence derives its meaning from and must be aligned with an idea that at once transcends and informs the actually given.

However, Platonism and prophetism also differ in several essential aspects. Whereas Plato's philosophy is based on a scientific mode of cognition, the ethical postulates of the prophets are anchored in their divinely revealed religious insights. And whereas Plato regards ethics as the science of morality, the prophet emphasizes what Cohen calls "the spirituality of morality."

Despite his systematically developed theory of ideas, Plato does not delineate an idea of man. True, he speaks of the philosopher-king as the ideal man who will attain the highest possible level of knowledge, an understanding of the nature of the good. But Plato fails to see what the prophets clearly envisaged: an image of man-as-such, endowed with an intellectual and moral potential that is his because he is a human being and not because he is a member of any particular nationality or class.

This prophetic image of man as embodiment of all humanity bears a substantive similarity to the thought of Kant, who considers man—any man—as an end in himself. Proceeding from this premise, Kant formulates his "categorical imperative," his idea of universal law, and his postulate for perpetual peace—all notions anticipated by prophetic ethics. Cohen draws an analogy too between the Jewish and Kantian views on the autonomy of man's will. Both Judaism and Kant see freedom as the precondition for all morality, and both are confident that the free man, that is, the knowledgeable man, will choose the good and thus become "the bearer of morality."

In Judaism, "the bearer of morality" tries, by his ethical conduct, to approximate God, the "archetype of all morality." This God, the "new" God conceived by the prophets, is the uniquely One. Early Greek philosophy already intuited a unifying principle behind the apparent fragmentation of the cosmos. But the similarity between Xenophanes' concept of cosmic unity and Judaism's concept of divine uniqueness is superficial. A comparison in depth shows that the notion of "unity," characteristic of pantheistic thinking, is conceptually inferior to the notion of "uniqueness" which characterizes monotheism. And in Cohen's view, only an uncompromising monotheism can propound the doctrine of that indivisible One and Only God who is the revealer of the indivisible one and only morality.

The Social Ideal as Seen by Plato and by the Prophets

Plato and the prophets constitute the two most important wellsprings of modern culture. But these springs also contain foreign admixtures—a fact that holds true for all sources of culture—which, however, are reworked and thus absorbed by the unequalled creativeness of the Platonic and the prophetic spirit. Plato as well as the prophets may therefore rightfully be considered unique examples of historical originality.

A social ideal represents a fusion of two basic components: a scientific mode of cognition and an ethics formalized as religion. Plato is and remains the symbol of the former, and the prophets are and remain that of the latter. The thrust of science reaches beyond the domain of nature into the realm of ethics; hence there is an intermingling of scientific and religious motives in Plato's work. And the prophets, though looking inward into the nature of morality, cannot help but look outward too at the reality of human existence. Thus, they are not entirely without mundane knowledge though they limit its horizon to the area of human concerns. But whereas Plato draws ethics into the cognitive sphere, the prophets remain strangers to the scientific realm. They are interested not in the totality of nature but only in the nature of man. . . .

Plato is above all interested in developing a theory of knowledge. He is neither the first Greek to undertake this task nor the first philosopher to link the problem of science to that of ethics. But it is he who turns the given data of knowledge into a science of knowledge by inquiring into the relation of science to epistemology.

In order to determine this relationship, he creates the theory of ideas. True, the idea itself springs as naturally and indigenously from the matrix of morality as from that of science. But the conceptual elaboration of the merely sensed or envisioned idea is accomplished exclusively within the context of science. . . .

With the inception of the idea and the creation of concepts, the naiveté of thinking as such comes to an end: aided by science and the method basic to science, the concept, or thinking as such, comes to understand itself.

What is the nature of the idea? This question permits of a definitive answer: the idea is a concept perceived by a scientific method of cognition, a mode of cognition closely linked to science if not derived from it.

Hence all idealism must be grounded in science. Without an unfailing adherence to the methodology of science there can be no cognitive knowledge, no idea, no idealism. An idealism that merely envisages and intuits is one-sided Platonism, to put it mildly. But Platonism is an absolutely coherent system and any one-sidedness would be inconsistent with its unity of thought.

The coherence of Platonism as well as the way in which it combines science with ethics, or ethics with science, account for its historical perpetuity. The idea—born as mathematical idea—matures into the idea of the good, a conceptual expansion silencing all skepticism. The good, to be sure, is not being as such, but this does not mean that it lacks the validity of an idea; it means rather that it is "beyond being."

The concept of transcendence originated not in connection with the idea of God but with that of the good. The idea of the good, though beyond being, is by no means beyond man's cognitive grasp. True, this idea has not sprung directly from a matrix of science. Nevertheless, a scientific mode of cognition is also a desideratum in the realm of ethics. That is, the ethical must be made a subject of scientific inquiry and thus become part of cognitive knowledge. . . .

Social consciousness regards prophetism as a pure source of religion. Yet we should also look at its limitations. The prophet knows nothing of science. Not even in Babylonia did he come under its spell, and in Palestine he certainly felt no inclination to lift its veil. The host of stars is of interest to him only because of the God who brought them into being, counted, and named them. Nature, by the same token, exists for him only as God's creation. The very first word of Genesis, "in the beginning," has a somewhat uncertain meaning, and this is characteristic. For the vagueness of the term would seem to indicate that any question about the material out of which God might have created heaven and earth is beyond the horizon of the Biblical mind, which can barely cope with the concept of chaos, let alone conceive of some primeval matter. Instead, we are here immediately presented—through a poetic view of nature—with a universe that appears before us with the finished products of water and light, plants and animals. Such a view of nature must preclude any interest in its possible control, and is not likely to make man doubt that sense perception really transmits a true picture of the world he sees. Nor does the Biblical mind examine the means of consciousness, e.g. the significance of thought as juxtaposed with emotion, or similar problems which arise once the difference between subject and object and their relation begin to dawn upon man.

All such inquiries are typical of a mind which sees reality as the seat of all truth. For the prophet, however, truth lies not in reality but in God, who created that reality but who can also change it, so that truth cannot inhere within nature itself. And herein lies the limitation of prophetic thinking. Unconcerned with science, it is equally unconcerned with the problem of cognitive knowledge.

All prophets speak of "knowledge of God," however, and the term does not seem ill-chosen. Yet if we maintain the methodological—or, in Greece, the historical—connection between knowledge and science, the term "knowledge of God" can be used only metaphorically. For the God of the prophets is beyond all sense perception, and any materiality constitutes a sharp contrast to His nature.

Given this fact, we can understand why the Hebrew genuis for language equates knowledge with love. True, the word "love" is here meant to express that inner sense of comprehension which borders on union. Nevertheless, the fact that the prophets equated knowledge with love and that it occurred to them to speak of love in connection with an unapproachable God would remain inexplicable were it not for their insight that it takes more than knowledge to "know" God. The contradistinction between their concept of God and anything that could be actually perceived or symbolically represented (hence also between knowledge and sense perception) was self-evident to them. Still, in order to eliminate any possible link between knowledge of God and knowledge of nature, they transmuted the former into love, a notion that has nothing whatever in common with science. But how can this prophetic concept of love, that is, love of and by God, be justified in positive terms?

The prophets are the originators not only of social religion but of social consciousness as such: borrowing the concept "love of God" from mysticism, they sought a path to understanding not through science but through love. But how could this be done? It could indeed not have been done had they concentrated their quest for knowledge or understanding on God alone. However, they did not stop there but instead established a link, a relationship, a correlation between God and man. And it was in this way that the postulate of love came into being; it originated in their thinking not about God but about man. It was man the prophets sought to understand, though not on the basis of any science of man. Plato, too, had no such science to aid him in his quest for knowledge. He therefore resorted to his idea, while the prophets resorted to their God.

It can surely not be assumed that the prophets, and they alone among the seers of all nations, arrived at their conception of the One God without speculation. But it is quite characteristic that their speculation about God as the uniquely One remained unsupported by science, and concerned itself not with metaphysics but with the problem of morality. And morality, in turn, is concerned with questions not about God but about man. For this reason, and from the very first, the Babylonian God, the creator of heaven and earth, was as such transformed into the God of man, the Creator of man.

But even though the prophets put God, in a manner of speaking, before the tribunal of man, they regard man neither as the son of gods nor as a demigod or hero. Their image of man is one of human weakness. And inasmuch as this weakness is primarily a moral inadequacy, the sinner is seen as archetypal man. Yet just as philosophy remains alien to prophetic ethics, so does a sense of tragedy. The prophets, therefore, do not dwell on guilt or punishment as the two aspects of a fate constituting the poetic ground of human existence. Rather than looking upon suffering as man's inescapable fate, they regard it as a stage in the development of mankind. Moreover, by eliminating this tragic concept, they also eradicate the elemental mythical notion of the envy of the gods. The God of the prophets is infinitely good; yet He is not the good as such. And though He may send suffering, this suffering does not represent evil as such. It is an integral part of that development of the good which is vouchsafed by the good God.

To sever the connection between suffering and guilt—to discard, that is, the notion that suffering is a punishment for guilt— is one of the most far-reaching consequences of monotheistic thinking, and of momentous significance for man's approach to the social problem. For the existence of suffering poses the most difficult question regarding God's goodness. But wherever man associates suffering primarily with death, mythology still reigns supreme. Here, death is depicted as a fate to which even the gods are subject. As long as mysticism dominates man's thought, his moral sense remains inert. If he is to awaken to his moral responsibility and take action against human suffering, he will have to learn to turn his glance away from the common destiny of illness and death, and begin to understand human misery not in biological but sociological terms. And thus the poor man becomes the symbol of all men.

The entire development of prophetism can be traced along these lines of thought. God is not the father of Israel's heroes, and it is not they who are called God's beloved. God loves the stranger. In the view of polytheism, the stranger—who, it is true, may on occasion become an honored guest—is the very opposite of the ideal man. The ideal man must be a member of one's own people. The stranger is the barbarian. But man's horizon widens as soon as he realizes that his own God also loves the barbarian and even declares that the hostile nations are quite as much His precious possession as is Israel itself.

Messianism demands and gives impetus to this development, which leads to cosmopolitanism. Here, however, we wish to examine another line of development, a line that leads to socialism.

Prophetism depicts God almost always as loving not only the stranger but also the orphan and the widow; they are therefore seen as victims of social oppression from which they will be liberated through God's justice. But though the prophets invoke justice and righteousness again and again, proclaiming their God as the God of righteousness, they are not really satisfied with this abstraction, which is actually a form of conceptualization. They wish to address man's heart, which they treasure more highly than his mind, and arouse his compassion as a mode of awareness commensurate with suffering. The Hebrew language has a unique term [*rahamim*, "compassion"] for this emotion, derived from *rehem* or "womb." God compassionately takes pity upon the poor; and man must compassionately discover his fellow man in the poor.

Consequently, compassion must not be regarded as an emotion, a physiological affect common to both man and beast; it is a spiritual factor, a surrogate of the spirit, one might say. As such, compassion becomes the motivating force of an entire *Welt-*

anschauung. One would have to despair of God's justice, goodness and providence were it not for this sense of compassion which furnishes man with whatever strength he needs to fight the skepticism his so-called mind produces. Of all the suffering man has to endure, his poverty ought to concern us most. It enslaves his very nature. If only poverty did not put its stamp on man and his world, he might conceivably be able to conquer even death itself. Moreover, it is a fateful fallacy to look upon poverty as punishment of man's guilt. With such faulty reasoning one will discover neither God's nor man's truth, nor even man himself. Only compassion will disclose to me the man in my fellow man. Through my sense of compassion, the other's suffering becomes my own, and the other becomes my fellow human being.

It is significant that Plato does not delineate an idea of man; and it is equally significant that it is Philo, the Jew, who takes this forward step in the theory of ideas. In his view, man merits being the object of knowledge as much as do mathematics or the world of nature. And the Platonic idea of the good does not satisfy Philo either. For even though Plato already posits a good God, this notion remains one-sided and not really thought through as long as man himself is not seen as good, actually or potentially. It was the prophets who discovered man's innate worth, and it is to their social conscience that we owe this discovery. They equated the poor and the righteous. This equation is decisive, representing a high mark in the development of Messianism. Subsequently the Messiah himself becomes the standard-bearer of poverty.[1] Taking upon himself all human guilt, he takes upon himself all human suffering. Devoid of the magic charm of heroic strength or godlike beauty, he rides through the world on his donkey, a symbol of human suffering. Disdaining all aesthetic attractions of the world, he represents, in his own social misery, the misery of man.

That Faustian poem of the Old Testament,[2] the Book of Job, also implies Messianic thinking. Having received the prophets' assurance that there is no causal relationship between any individ-

1. See "The Style of the Prophets," p. 118 f.
2. Cohen's usage, though this is the Christian terminology; Jews speak of the Hebrew Bible.

ual's suffering and the conduct of his ancestors, man still asks: "But what causes human evil"? Instead of posing this metaphysical question, he should learn to ask: "What causes human suffering"? The answer, negatively expressed, is that poverty is not a punishment for guilt. Positively expressed, however, this Biblical answer leads to the growing realization that the poor man should actually be acknowledged as the good man. No preconceived notion of God or man and no worldly experience should cause us to question the validity of this insight. The God of the prophets is the God of justice, and will therefore somehow help the poor. He is the God of world history, and therefore, will at some time make amends to mankind for the suffering of the individual. And He is the God of kindness, so that it must be considered an act of kindness when He inflicts the misery of poverty upon man. As he thus realizes God's goodness, man will come to think of the poor as the righteous, the God-fearing and His favorites.

True, this Biblical insight is not derived from any science and therefore does not represent the idea of the good. Nor is it a notion of some abstract good and transferable as such to material goods. It is a reflection upon the nature of the good as it becomes manifest in man, concretely and personally. For it is only in man that the love of God is kindled.

Now, we ought to admit the limitations of this kind of thinking and of this concept of God and of man. True, it was compassion with suffering that led to the development of these views; but it is self-evident that so limited an insight could not obliterate the metaphysics of death. Man always prefers pious reveries to good deeds. We certainly understand that the proddings of even limited religious insights serve to check and control man's demonic nature and motivate him to perform some good deeds. Yet we also understand that compassion alone is not an adequate motivation for social action. In the final analysis, our moral problems will be assured of solution only if we apply to them whatever new insights we can derive from the sources of science, sources that must be continuously deepened and freshened. And thus we must once again turn from the prophets to Plato.

The fact that Plato makes knowledge the basic principle of his system constitutes its greatest advantage. Human compassion is no substitute for knowledge. Without philosophy, mankind's suffering cannot be ended; knowledge must become the cornerstone of the world's social structure. Without it, the cause of man's misery will never be found, let alone eliminated; nor will man be redeemed from his suffering. Prophetic insight is merely a vision after all, an intuition; and it is a real shortcoming that prophetism fails to substantiate this intuition methodologically. Moreover, it is a shortcoming of religion as such not to submit its teachings to the methodology of science as a matter of principle. Though it conceives of the human mind as the God-given "holy spirit," [3] religion shies away from ascribing to scientific insights the same validity as to divinely revealed ethical insights. Yet we cannot really speak of truth in the entire realm of religion unless we acknowledge, without reservation, that all moral cognition must also be scientifically or philosophically substantiated. And here the divine Plato, admonishing us to pursue the eternal verities, remains forever the guardian of a scientific approach to knowledge as the only infallible guarantee of truth.

Having looked at the light that illuminates Platonism, however, we must now also contemplate its dark side. The well-known statement that there will be no end to human suffering until "kings will be philosophers, and philosophers kings" already discloses the shadow thrown by this light. To be sure, we should not be offended by the term "kings" but take it simply as a designation for those charged with governing. But must we assume that the sharp division of men into those who govern and those who are governed is really to be perpetuated forever? Should not all men, at some future time, participate in their government, so that all will be rulers as well as the ruled? And is it really conceivable that Plato should have failed to realize that this postulate is a necessary corollary of the principle that knowledge ought to be accessible to all men endowed with reason? . . .

The flaw in a system which regards intellect and reason as the sole principles of cognition here becomes so manifest that one feels tempted to resort, after all, to the frail principle of compas-

3. See "The Holy Spirit."

sion. Scientifically speaking, we see here the ambiguity of Plato's concept of reason (insofar as this, intrinsically, is moral reason, and as such identical with scientific reason and grounded in it). For his statement about the philosopher-kings implies that since not all men have the faculty to understand science (why not?), they also lack the faculty to understand philosophy. And inasmuch as all morality must be grounded in an understanding of philosophy, all those who lack this understanding also lack the basis for acting morally. Hence they must be governed by rulers, that is, by philosophers.

This consequence of Plato's thought is consistent with the principle of his theory of ideas, at least to the extent to which he himself could bring the idea of the good into accord with his general theory of ideas. But no advantage of his system can compensate for the damage the world has suffered because of Plato's over-extension of his methodological principle. Even today's skepticism with regard to any social ideal feeds on the prejudice that not all men have the aptitude to pursue knowledge scientifically, and that therefore this avenue to an understanding of morality must remain closed to them.

It becomes clear then that Plato's idea of man is inconsistent. For without the basic notion that all men are equally endowed with reason, there can be no all-encompassing concept of man. And without such a concept, there can be no faith in mankind's eventual realization of the idea of morality. But how meaningful is a scientifically reasoned idealism which does not arrive at the conclusion that all mankind must be one, that there must be no class distinctions anywhere, and that all men have the potential to comprehend, hence to achieve the good? In short, what point is there to an idealism which does not recognize that every man's mind can harbor the idea of the good?

Here, it becomes clear why prophetism, though one-sided and lacking scientific foundation, has a practical advantage over Platonism. For prophetism tolerates no discrimination against men, and no differentiation among them. This is illustrated by the simple rule which prescribes that not only every ordinary man but even the king—once the people desire a king—must copy, by his own hand, the book of divine teachings. Thus the king and every man in the nation are put on the same level: as far as the relationship between God and man is concerned, there must be no distinction between ruler and ruled, between philosophers and non-philosophers. Moses' exclamation: "Would that all the Lord's people were prophets!" (Numbers 11:29) implies a distinction between the actuality of the present and the potentiality of the future but none concerning the quality of the human mind. Hence, Jeremiah's statement that in the future no one will have to teach anyone else because everybody, great and small, will know God. All men are promised the fullness of moral knowledge: the fullness, for this knowledge is rooted in the principle of God which, though surely not one of scientific cognition, is a coherent, dual principle comprising God as well as man. . . .

The prophets are no philosophers.[4] For them, it suffices that men acquire a knowledge of God and, through God, of man. Confident that all men are capable of such knowledge, they would despair of God if their confidence were ever shaken. Their optimism constitutes the advantage of their idealism—if we may apply to their thinking this term in the sense suggested by common usage. However, their notion of "knowledge of God" is limited to moral teachings; and inasmuch as these are not grounded in scientific knowledge, they should not, in precise terminology, be referred to as ethics.

Broadly speaking, we might say that world history fluctuates between these two basic orientations, the Platonic and the prophetic, with their conflicts as well as their interactions. In our time, we must gain a twofold insight. First, we must understand that any pessimism concerning the ability of the so-called masses to engage in scholarship is a basic evil inhibiting and making illusory all true progress. "All the people a nation of priests"—this fundamental prophetic principle must become the motto of the new world.

Secondly, the preconceived notion should be abolished that all morality must be grounded in or promoted by religion alone. Plato is wrong only in his denial of the masses' capacity to understand philosophy. But he is right in foreseeing that there can be no peace

4. See "The Style of the Prophets."

on earth without an ethics substantiated by philosophy. We must therefore fully support that social theory which consistently demands that school and state make scientific instruction available to the entire population. The substantive no less than the pedagogical foundation of all higher scientific instruction was, is, and will continue to be philosophy, which, fusing logic and ethics, represents the sole basis of idealism.

Even today, therefore, the prophets as well as Plato remain the spiritual guides of mankind. And we shall have to make use of both prophetic and Platonic insights if we are to reach the goal suggested by their social ideal.

Affinities Between the Philosophy of Kant and Judaism

The inner affinities between Kant's philosophy and Judaism are evident in the substantive similarity between the ethics of the Kantian system and the basic ideas of Judaism, though Kant himself neither intended nor was even aware of any such accord. . . .

These affinities might be supposed to derive from the ethics of Judaism alone; for Judaism has no science and therefore no logic— that is, no science or logic within a philosophical system. Judaism did try, however, and even quite early, to validate its teachings through philosophy. In this way the concept of logos came into being. And because an attempt to undergird Judaism with an ethics had been made ever since Saadyah [1] in the tenth century and possibly even before, it was inevitable that this ethics should also be provided with some sort of logical foundation. Thus, some inner accord between these early efforts of Judaism and the Kantian method can already be recognized here.

1. Saadyah ben Joseph (882–942), head or Gaon of the Academy at Sura, Babylonia.

Kant's thought is characterized, in a fundamental and decisive way, by a certain passage in his *Critique of Pure Reason*. He says there that all cognition must be based on principles which are to be regarded as basic truths. This is what the concept "reason," particularly "pure reason," signifies, in contradistinction to sense perception and empirical knowledge (insofar as the latter consists of an accumulation of such perceptions). To accept sense perceptions as the ultimate ground of knowledge is to relinquish any claim to an objective basis of knowledge as represented, for instance, by the axioms of mathematics. For believers in miracles and spiritualists invoke sense experience, and literalists accept the sense datum of the written word as their criteria of truth. But those who would make reason their criterion of truth must apply this principle to the study of Holy Scriptures as well. And our devout philosophers of reason have actually done no less.

Maimonides [2] was by no means the first of them to use the Aristotelian rational principle as a guideline for his religious writings. Saadyah, too, had already formulated this rule clearly and distinctly in his *Emunot ve-Deot*.[3] For Aristotle, all knowledge is based on the most abstract principle as well as on sense perception. (Despite if not actually because of this dualism he was more comprehensible to the Middle Ages than Kant proved to be to the period immediately following his own. The great minds of his own time, in whatever fields of endeavor, had clearly understood him. But he remained unintelligible to the romanticism that spread soon thereafter because its obscurantism prevented any real confrontation with his thought.) To our ancient thinkers, Aristotle's dualism was rather welcome, though not because of its theoretical ambiguity. But they themselves always emphasize reason and are not in the least concerned with the conflict between reason and sense experience. What matters to them is the distinction between reason and revelation.

This distinction, however, by no means implies a conflict be-

2. Also known as *Rambam,* an acronym for Rabbi Moses ben Maimon (1135–1204); religious philosopher and codifier (as well as court physician in Egypt); major works: *Mishneh Torah* (a codification of Jewish law); *Moreh Nevukhim* [*Guide of the Perplexed*].
3. *Beliefs and Opinions,* considered a Jewish philosophical classic.

tween those two sources of religion. Nor should it lead to the conclusion that revelation has nothing to do with ethics, or that it concerns merely ritual legislation (with the possible inclusion of state legislation). Such a conclusion would not do justice to the high regard in which religious consciousness holds revelation. And ritual legislation, far from conflicting with ethics, is understood to serve as its vehicle. (This is where Paulinism, today as always, becomes subjective and therefore unjust, no matter how correct its judgment about the value of all particularistic religious practices might be in principle.)

Ancient Judaism regards the difference between moral and ritual legislation somewhat like that between pure and practical ethics. Subsequently, both are seen as legitimate subjects of revelation, as is moral reason—though the latter is also considered autonomous. And Saadyah significantly states that no real discussion is possible with anyone who asserts that only the Torah, and not also reason, is a source of ethics. This shows how unreservedly reason is upheld as a controlling principle of the Torah.

Similarly, there is a statement in Bahya ibn Pakuda's *Duties of the Heart* [4] to the effect that man's blind acceptance of revelation as the sole source of knowledge, to the exclusion of his own reasoning power, might well be the work of his evil inclination. Thus, reason, that inexhaustible and indispensable source of all morality, is acknowledged as the inviolable basis of religion. And it would not take too much to go on from here to an acknowledgment of the sovereignty of reason, as long as revelation is not assigned a secondary position and its sovereignty also remains inviolate.

The decisive factor, though, in determining the sovereignty of reason is one's concept of reason's relation to the world of the senses. And here we encounter another affinity between the philosophy of Judaism and that of Kant.

Kant's ethics is characterized, above all, by its rejection of eudaemonism [5] and all its variations. He contends that all eudae-

4. A guide to Jewish, spiritual living. Bahya ben Joseph ibn Pakuda lived in the late 11th century in Moslem Spain.
5. A philosophical theory which regards man's attainment of happiness and well-being (through the fullest realization of his intellectual and physical potential) as motivation and goal for all his aspirations.

monic moral systems contradict the concept of ethics and that the pure will must never aspire to any kind of happiness. And since Jewish philosophy also unequivocally rejects the principle of happiness—from Saadyah to Maimonides and beyond—we are surely justified to note, at this point, yet another agreement between the Jewish and the Kantian view.

This opposition to any eudaemonic principle is at once a sign of the Jewish mind's autonomy and ability to systematize and a most interesting symptom of Biblical thinking. For it is always the Bible that serves these thinkers as the last criterion by which to judge their own views. Even concerning the role of reason they invoke the Torah, which repeatedly speaks of knowledge as fundamental to all matters of the human heart, mind, and volition. "Know this day, and lay it to thy heart . . ." (Deuteronomy 4:39). And in keeping with the spirit of the Torah, they consider even scientific knowledge as a basic requirement for human understanding. For mathematics, astronomy and ethics all have a common foundation in reason. And as for the question of eudaemonism, there is an abundance of Biblical sources. More telling than any quotes, though, is that basic tenet of faith, the unity of God, whose corollaries are "unity of the heart" and "unity of action."

It would seem that no language has a more meaningful expression to convey the concept of man's integrity than this "unity of the heart." This profound and crystal-clear leitmotif taken from the Psalms—"Make one my heart to fear thy name" (Psalms 86:11)—also informs our prayers with its harmoniousness and enhances our Days of Repentance. Unity of the heart is the prerequisite for love and veneration of God. "Unify our hearts so that we may love and venerate Your name"—had Baḥya's *Duties of the Heart* disclosed to us no other concept than that of a unity of heart, action and veneration of God, this alone would suffice to make it a work of considerable value.

Set against the principles of pleasure and happiness is the principle of reason, that reason of volition which overcomes any schism and establishes the unity of the will. To Kant, however, this kind of unity (namely, unity of heart and mind) would still be suspect as a merely psychological definition. For he seeks to define the moral will by objective, conceptual principles. Refusing to accept the pleasure principle as the causative factor of volition, he posits a logically derived concept as the determining principle of the will: universal law. Morality must be regarded as a law valid for any individual, without exception. True, this law is seen as derived from the autonomy of reason; but reason's only relation to the will is to impose upon it a universal law. We must not be "volunteers of morality." Kant might have learned this expression from a Jewish philosopher or from the Talmud itself: "Greater is the man who acts in obedience to the commandment than without commandment" (*Kiddushin* 31 a).

Here, however, we must not overlook an essential difference between the Kantian and Jewish positions. In the final analysis, in Kant, it is reason itself which must create the universal law anew. But in Judaism, the One God would become a useless machine were He not the eternal source of moral law. Judaism simply denies any possible conflict between the concepts of God and of moral reason. Moral law must and can be both: the law of God and the law of reason.

God and His law signify as well as establish a contrast with the individual's egotism and self-centeredness, or simply with his limited horizon. And this interpretation of law constitutes still another affinity between Judaism and Kant. In the final analysis, we have here the ancient idea of men's equality before God, which finds its methodological expression in the concept of a universal law. This same basic concept underlies the original commandment to love one's fellow man. Maybe its correct translation should read: "Love him; he is like you."

Actually, the difference between Kant's and Judaism's view concerning the autonomy of the moral law only points up another accord between them. For though Kant upholds the autonomy of the moral law, he does not at all deny the existence of God, to whom he refers as "the sovereign in the realm of morals." Thus, self-legislation of human reason in no way implies, let alone impels, an abdication of this sovereign. Kant simply recognizes no realm of morality without God, the Sovereign. But what is the task assigned to God in the administration of morality?

It is well known that this question touches upon one of the weakest points in Kant's system. We may here disregard the fact that Kant, completely contradicting himself, makes God the "distributor of happiness," so that the imbalance of our earthly existence might be righted in the beyond. This argument is nothing but a medieval turn of speech, and atypical for Kant. Though he had rid himself, on logical grounds, of the idea this phrase represents, it somehow still remained part of him, marking him as a child of his time.

What is really characteristic of Kant's view of God, however, is his concept of a non-personal, truly spiritual dimension: the sublimation of God into the Idea. And this is nothing less than the core-meaning of the Jewish God-idea too.

It is particularly difficult to show how compellingly convincing this thesis is just because it expresses what is most profound and true, and indeed what is the ultimate that can be known of God. Man prefers to think of God in material terms, though these serve merely to pave the way for the triumph of atheism. Yet our intellectual history teaches us at every turn, and the concept of God's unity makes it mandatory: monotheism as monotheism must be informed by the Idea.

The campaign of our later exegetes and philosophers against physical, material, or mythological conceptions of God is already anticipated by early opposition to the anthropomorphisms found in the Bible. Even the question whether God can be said to be "alive" is not new in Maimonides' writings, though it is boldly and precisely formulated there. Saadyah had already been disturbed by this problem. As a matter of principle, God's being must be different from all other kinds of being, hence also from "being alive."

The teachings about God's attributes furnish important and convincing proof for this fundamental trend in Jewish thought (which reflects a uniform orientation all along the line). Here, Maimonides becomes the guide of the perplexed even for those who do not realize they are perplexed. Nicolas of Cusa cannot quote him enough, and he influenced Leibniz too. And Spinoza derives the basic principle for his definition of substance from Saadyah. Still, what a profound ethical difference between Maimonides or Saad-yah and Spinoza! For the former, it is legitimate to make state-ments about God's moral attributes alone, that is, those attributes which bear upon man's actions. And neither man nor any God-man, but only God and God alone can be acknowledged as the exemplar of those actions.

God's essence is morality, and morality only; this and nothing else is divine nature. Physical nature, however, is God's creation. God is not nature. Though His being is not in conflict with that of nature (which is below the level of good and evil), it is wholly distinct from it. And it is this distinction from nature which is im-plied in the concept of divine Oneness.[6]

The close resemblance between Judaism and Kant's religious thought is also evidenced by the fact that Kant, when writing about the Trinity—a concept for which he had to make allowances owing to the political tendency of his religious essay—recognizes the Son only and then equates him with the idea of mankind. Scho-lasticism had already interpreted the Trinity in moral and psy-chological terms, which points up a certain liberating trend in the reasoning of the Middle Ages. The pantheistic structure of roman-ticism, however, rests on the dogma of God's incarnation. God is man, for God is nature as such—a dogma which here becomes the guiding principle of all metaphysics and certainly not of ethics alone. But ethics is thereby actually eliminated as a separate dis-cipline, for it is absorbed into the general process of natural be-coming.

This is the hidden poison indiscriminately swallowed by those who, though otherwise well educated, do not know how to discern the basic logical errors constituting the premise of pantheism. God is neither man nor is He nature. The very meaning of all creation is to be a vehicle for morality. Yet created nature can never be in conflict with the laws of mathematics. Even God's omnipotence is delimited by mathematical and logical reason. This too is a basic concept of our ancient thinkers, and has direct bearing upon any theory of miracles. Pantheism, however, considers nature and morality as belonging to the same norm. Divesting moral reason of

6. See "Uniqueness Rather Than Unity of God."

its uniqueness and autonomy, it leaves theoretical reason in the twilight of symbolism.

It is nothing short of amazing to discover here a still closer relationship between Kant and Judaism. In his system, Kant distinguishes ethics from logic. Both are derived from reason; yet there is, in Kant's view, a difference between practical—that is, moral—and theoretical reason. Maimonides deals with this issue in a similar way, and the maturity and originality of his thought, distinguishing him from his predecessors, become nowhere so evident as at this point. Granted, he too assigns morality to "the first principles of reason." Nevertheless, his "exact proof" demonstrates the difference between moral and logical-mathematical principles.

Here, our great Moses exhibits brilliant lucidity that does much to illuminate both the logical-scientific and the ethical side of the question. Morality and its principles are neither the equivalent of science and logic nor their equal. There is indeed a methodological difference between ethics and mathematics. Yet reason remains their common ground, so that Maimonides can combine his "service of the heart" with the principles of reason.

The God of Judaism is the God of transcendence. This notion is offensive to pantheism, which considers the God dwelling in my heart as superior—as if God did not dwell in my heart, in the purity of my heart, precisely because He is enthroned above any powers of my own! God's immaterialness is an absolute prerequisite for His moral efficaciousness; that is, it provides the basis for the establishment of morality in all of mankind and sets up a goal for world history. But wherever God and man, or God and nature are equated, mysticism inevitably ensues. It turns the moral into the supernatural, and the supernatural into the natural. It romantically confuses the true meaning of morality, obscuring, with its superstition, man's natural, sensate existence.

The notion of immortality is linked to the God-idea; both constitute a border problem of the material world. It is well known that Kant, though excluding both the notion of immortality and the God-idea from the truly knowable, retained both as concepts of moral cognition. And all of Judaism's statements on human dignity and the value of human life reflect a sense of confidence, a hope for immortality. "I know that my redeemer liveth." This hope was alive in Jewish literature long before Job, and therefore is not bound up with the literal meaning of the Jobean verse. In the main, both Kant and Jewish tradition consider the concept of immortality necessary because of its implicit notion of moral retribution.

But what is only natural for a philosopher who has been molded by the Enlightenment of the eighteenth century is a glorious achievement for medieval Jewish philosophy of religion and the Rabbinic literature closely related to it. The Jewish mind approaches all questions of the beyond with a certain reticence and discretion. No punishment of hell is threatened here: repentance will always redeem the sinner. Reward, too, is depicted in spiritual terms only; and mysticism is touched upon merely tangentially.

Yet it would be a misinterpretation of this reticence and a misjudgment of the psychology of the Jewish heart and mind if one were to assume that we take death lightly. Caring profoundly for our loved ones whose lives we share, we experience a grievous sense of bereavement at their passing, and our longing for them is great.

Still, we consider it both moving and inspiring when as religiously devout a poet as the author of the *Kuzari,* Yehuda Halevi,[7] holds that we can say no more about immortality and resurrection than what has been promised and guaranteed us by the psalmist: "But as for me, the nearness of God is my good" (Psalms 73:28). Even in the beyond, the Jew expects no other good than that constituted by the proximity of God, the Infinitely Good. Nor do the horrors of hell hold sway over his pious imagination. Immortality remains for him what it must remain for anyone with a sound understanding of the nature of ethics: a moral hope.

The third of the ideas posited by Kant is freedom. Freedom as human autonomy (of which we have already spoken) constitutes the basis of his ethics. The problem of human autonomy dominates all of medieval philosophy, hence also our philosophy of religion. A purely theoretical discussion of freedom would therefore point out some remarkable analogies between the Kantian and the Jew-

7. Poet and philosopher of religion; c. 1083–1141, Spain.

ish views. Here, though, where we are dealing with general questions only, we shall simply state that we find it characteristic that Ḥasdai Crescas,[8] whom Spinoza explicitly quotes as denying man's autonomy, actually retains the concept of freedom as a precondition for all morality. For Crescas, as similarly for Spinoza, "love of God" implies freedom of choice. And the passage from Deuteronomy, "choose life," [9] represents to him the commandment to accept the responsibility of freedom. This seeming contradiction need not disturb us. What is meant here is that God is the legislator of morality, and that He commands that man choose. But by choosing the good, man uses his moral faculty and thus exercises his freedom.

It is significant, however, that no mention is made of a certain passage characterizing the sinner as one who chooses evil. By de-emphasizing though not precluding this negative alternative—the freedom to choose evil—the positive alternative is made to appear as the only one worth considering. Actually, freedom is understood to mean nothing but purity of soul. And this interpretation represents another unmistakable resemblance to the thought of Kant. . . .

Through his purity of soul, man becomes the image of God. Man is not holy. To think of man as holy seems blasphemous to us. But man is pure; his soul is pure. The purity of his soul is an infallible mark of man's immortality and exemplifies his freedom.

Kant's idea of freedom leads to an additional notion: the concept of the "end in itself" or the "final goal," which is represented by man himself. One wonders how pantheism, if it has any rational tendency whatever, can possibly undertake to improve upon the meaning expressed by the idea that man is the world's final purpose. As the bearer of morality, man bestows upon nature meaning and inner cohesion.

The forces of nature, though regulated by profoundly impressive mathematical laws, provide a satisfactory answer to man's quest for meaning only when he considers himself more than their tool

8. C. 1340–1410, Spain; philosopher of religion who criticized the Aristotelian rationalist tradition in Jewish thought, as exemplified by Maimonides.
9. ". . . . I have set before Thee life and death, the blessing and the curse; therefore choose life. . . ." (Deuteronomy 30:19).

or toy. The world's ultimate meaning must be morality. This is what is meant by the assertion that man is the world's final purpose. The same idea is clearly and distinctly expressed by Saadyah. And it is for this reason that Maimonides posits self-perfection rather than happiness as the governing principle of man's life. Even the concept of an "end in itself" does not have a more profound significance.

Translated into practical terms, this concept suggests that every individual represents such an end and must therefore never be used merely as a means. And this most profound and clear meaning of the categorical imperative is deeply ingrained in the Jew. In fact, we all know that even those who have only the most superficial knowledge of Judaism find sufficient reason for denouncing it as an ancient source of romantic dreams of freedom and equality.

The prophets would not have become the wellspring of all genuine political morality had they not aggressively taught, and indeed shed their blood for, this notion of man as an end in himself. The social legislation of the Pentateuch, that greatest creation of socio-ethical idealism which has not remained a Utopia, is due to their activity. The Sabbath has conquered the world; it is a symbol of the idea that even as a laborer man must remain an end in himself. His final purpose as a human being is not realized when he remains a cog in civilization's machinery, especially if that civilization fails to extend its benefits to him in the same measure and to the same degree as to any other man. The symbol of the Sabbath with its motto: ". . . that thy man-servant and thy maid-servant may rest as well as thou" (Deuteronomy 5:14) cannot be said to be less explicit than any philosophical concept; surely it has not been less effective.

Judaism's social idealism is related to its Messianism. Here, the close affinity to Kant is quite obvious. Kant wrote an essay on "Perpetual Peace," showing that the idea of universality is basic not only to his ethics but also to his view on history. History would seem incomprehensible to him if it did not have a goal. This goal, he says, is perpetual peace, and even wars are being waged so as to promote this peace. . . .

The first to conceive of the idea of universal peace and place their confidence in it as world history's purpose and meaning were the prophets; indeed, it is this concept that made them true teachers of the love for one's fellow man. War is the Satan of world history. To think, as the ancient Greeks did, that war is the father of the world, representing the true meaning of life and the inevitable fate of nations and individuals, is both a mockery of the idea of God as father of all men and a contradiction of the concept of man as an end in himself and as final purpose. He who believes in perpetual peace believes in the Messiah, and not in a Messiah who has already come but in one who must and will come. . . .

The Jewish philosopher must experience a sense of special affinity with Kant. For the Kantian system is based on the logic of science and is characterized by the primacy of ethics. And ethics is also the most vital principle of Judaism, whose religion wants to be and indeed is moral teaching. Love of God means knowledge of God. And knowledge of God means awareness of mankind's moral goal.

There is, then, an innermost accord between the systematic dispositions of Kant and the basic orientation of prophetic Judaism. Judaism has constantly renewed itself out of its prophetic sources. And its philosophy of religion would suffer from an inner conflict with the Rabbinic ritualism it retains if its prophetic character did not seek to assert itself everywhere, claiming priority for its own spiritual values and establishing a preponderance of them.

This, in fact, constitutes the difference between philosophy of religion and history of religion: the former knows how to construe the essence of a religion through the conceptual idealization of its basic thought, while the latter disqualifies itself when it declares that it depicts the essence of religion. It is neither the historian's task, nor does he have the competence to define essence. He may acknowledge that some phenomena are of merely secondary importance; but as far as his research is concerned, he cannot regard any of them as non-essential. Only philosophy of religion can accept the responsibility to decide what is and what is not essential in any given religion.

And historical developments prove ever more distinctly and definitively that the idealization undertaken by our philosophy of religion is correct. Judaism's value—even for the development of Protestantism—as represented by its prophetism (hence, its ethics), its universalism, and its humanism is already widely acknowledged today. And as for its ritualism, we regard this as part of its historical development, as a consequence of its need for self-defense and self-protection, and thus as part of the imponderables of religious piety (which, by the way, is the source of all poetry as well as the inspiration of all human history). Nevertheless, we do make a clear and vital, though possibly still somewhat embarrassed distinction between the ritualism of our religion and its eternal essence.

The inner justification and cultural impact of our religion stem from the rightness of its moral ideas; and there is comfort and hope for us in the fact that those ideas are so closely related to and in full accord with the exemplary ethics of the new era ushered in by the French Revolution. The mystics and obscurantists who would pass off some so-called poetry for philosophy will eventually be driven away, along with other misguided spirits of this accursed and confused age. Classical thinking will once again awaken in philosophy as well as in art; and from it there will emerge a new direction in politics. Akin to the moral purity of prophetic monotheism, this new political orientation will come to acknowledge and appreciate Judaism as its most natural ally.

Let us be sure, therefore, not to lose our innate Messianic optimism. The evil spirits, in league with pessimism, will vanish once again. Moral soundness, human lucidity and integrity and, along with them, the creative cultural force of our eternally young religion will be universally acknowledged as surely as progress towards the realization of the good is and remains world history's goal.

This ultimate idea of the philosophy of history constitutes the common ground for Kantianism and Judaism: a philosophy whose truth is its methodology, and a religion whose truth is its God.

Uniqueness Rather Than Unity of God

I. UNITY VERSUS UNIQUENESS

Unity serves as the most fundamental and universal implement of thought. Thinking as such is a unifying process that pulls together the diverse elements of which any thought-material is composed. In fact, any such material, offered to the mind by perception and all forms of representation, is transformed into thought-substance only by this unifying mental process. Unity, therefore, is a constitutive characteristic of the mind.

It is of fundamental significance, particularly for the history of religious thought, that the concept of unity makes its first appearance in philosophy in conjunction with the idea of God. Xenophanes [1] was the first Greek thinker to link these two notions of unity and God. But it is equally significant that he introduced the mediating term "world" into this nexus.

Being the first to see the cosmos as a unified whole, Xenophanes liberated his thinking from the fragmentizing impact the multiplicity of phenomena has upon man's world view. Out of multiplicity and multifariousness, he intuited unity. Moreover, and most amazingly, he did not stop at this newly-won insight of a cosmic unity but went on to transfer this notion to the concept of God. The unity of the cosmos, he said, is God.

This is what tradition relates to us. But how can one explain that Xenophanes was not satisfied with discerning the unity of the cosmos—thereby preparing the ground for ideation as such—but that he applied the principle of unity, that great insight of his, to the (until then mythological) problem of God? By envisaging the

---

1. A pre-Socratic Greek philosopher to whom Aristotle refers, in his *Metaphysics,* as "the first partisan of the One" because he denied the existence of anthropomorphic gods and saw instead a divine principle of oneness permeating the entire cosmos.

unity of God and not merely that of the world, Xenophanes became the precursor of monotheism in Greek thought. In contradistinction to a world of mythology—and deriding the Greeks' most cherished art form of sculpture and its idealized gods—he teaches the idea of God's unity as represented, against a heavenful of gods, by Zeus. . . .

It is important to remember, however, that Xenophanes does not think of the two entities, world and God, as existing side by side. He fuses them into one unified whole. Thus merged, world and God become identical.

This preliminary stage of monotheism, then, is conducive to the rise of pantheism. True, monotheism and pantheism are in no way equivalent. But at this classical point, we can see the danger inherent in the concept of unity, inasmuch as it establishes a basic principle not merely for the world but for both world and God together. When world and God become one, unity turns into identity (which represents another basic principle of thought). Hence, it becomes clear at this point of Greek speculation that the idea of God's unity leads directly to pantheism. And this, in turn, discloses the important fact that the term unity cannot adequately convey the central idea of monotheism.

Biblical sources, to be sure, do not have a fully developed methodological philosophy; yet they contain the first rudiments of religious speculation. Inasmuch as they wish to disclose God's truth, how could it be otherwise? And how could the idea of God be formulated if not by a mode of thinking distinct from all sense perception? But since only conceptual thinking can convey any knowledge of God's being and its distinctiveness from all other forms of being in heaven as well as on earth, the idea of unity had to emerge even in these earliest sources in order to reveal the God of spirituality as the God of truth, over against the multiplicity of gods and sensate existence.

Furthermore, it is established already at this earliest crossroads of the mind that religious speculation does not simply imitate philosophy but proceeds along its own lines of thought, even with regard to universals. Religious speculation therefore rejects the concept of unity, that most universal medium of thought, replacing it with the concept of uniqueness. And with this, it envisages the new God.

God is the uniquely One—this is the new idea with which monotheism both makes its entrance into the world and refutes any view that merely acknowledges the principle of unity but disregards the concept of uniqueness. In the Greek view, as pointed out before, the universe, though consisting of an infinite number of worlds, had unity. What meaning, the Greeks might have asked, could there be in the concept of uniqueness, in addition to or beyond the significance implied by our notion of unity? But monotheism might easily pose a counter-question: Is the principle of unity really equally applicable to the world and to God? And does divine unity really imply merely a numerical concept, that is, a unity rather than a plurality of gods? This counter-question already infers that unity cannot be an adequate principle of monotheism: God must become the uniquely One.

This position seems to create a paradox for monotheism, however. What does the concept of God's unique Oneness actually signify if God and world are not seen as a unified entity? Does this mean that divine Oneness [that is, the singularity of divine being] denies the world any right whatever? And if so, which right? Obviously, the right to be even an object of thought; for it would seem as if God alone were the true subject matter of all thinking. But is it really true that monotheism regards nature in the negative terms of nihilism? Above all, is not man himself part of nature? And can God's unique Oneness therefore really, and in every sense, imply the nothingness of man as well as that of nature?

If this were the case, pantheism would indeed be the inescapable consequence, and monotheism would have to concede defeat. But if monotheism is to assert its validity against pantheism, and if Xenophanes' first word about that one [2] God is not also to be the last word spoken about Him, then divine Oneness must imply more than the merely negative notion that God alone can be the only valid subject matter of all thinking.

Biblical sources, as mentioned before, do not speculate about the nature of thinking. But their attempt to go beyond sense per-

2. See footnote [1] in "Religious Postulates," p. 55.

ception and to grasp the nature of conceptual thinking by trying to discern its authentic content and substance becomes evident in their idea of being—a notion no less basic to conceptual thought than unity and identity, the two concepts already discussed.

Xenophanes had conceived the idea of unity with regard to the cosmos but had applied it to the notion of one God. Then came Parmenides, who, though maintaining the principle of cosmic unity, did not transmute it into the idea of God. Instead, he transposed it into that other basic concept of thinking: being. From here on, the problem of philosophy is no longer the cosmos but being. Being and thinking now become correlative concepts of philosophic speculation.

It seems nothing short of a miracle that the Bible's earliest monotheistic thinking, though still non-conceptual, could deal with the problem of being. And yet, can there be any doubt about it, in view of the fact that the new God is given no other name than that derived from the notion of being?

When God first reveals Himself out of the midst of the burning bush, Moses asks Him what he should reply when the children of Israel question him about the God who has sent him and about His name. Whereupon God answers: *"I am that I am. . . .* Thus shalt thou say unto the children of Israel: *I am* hath sent me unto you" (Exodus 3:14).

Truly, there probably is no greater miracle in man's entire intellectual history than that disclosed by this sentence. Here, a primeval language, emerging without any philosophical concepts, stammers the most profound word of any philosophy. God's name, it says, is "I am that I am." God is the One Who Is. God is the I that signifies being as such.

It is characteristic that this being is designated not as a neuter but as an I. But should we therefore assume that being, by becoming the I That Is, the subject that is, loses its conceptual value of being as such?

Earlier, we inquired into the meaning of the concept of uniqueness [or Oneness] as it refers to God. Now we learn that the uniquely One God does in fact imply a singular mode of being, namely that of the Only One Who Is. And that brings us once again to the question whether monotheism does not turn into nihilism with regard to the world in general and man in particular. Does the concept of the One and Only God, in the sense of the Only One Who Is, really nullify all other modes of being? Or should we not rather say that God's unique being is merely distinct from any and all other modes of being in the world, including that of man? . . .

When the One God revealed Himself to Moses, He also issued His mandate to the people. It would therefore be paradoxical, and in fact not just a logical but also a psychological contradiction to think of the One God in terms of a nihilism that would deny any true being to world and man. The concept of unity does imply such a contradiction; the concept of uniqueness does not. Instead, we shall see that the latter actually precludes any such paradox, for it is predicated on the recognition that world and man do indeed exist, though their mode of being is not identical with God's unique mode of being.

A definition of this other mode of being—the world's and man's—will have to be inferred from God's being. And from this inference there will emerge the positive significance of the uniqueness of divine being.

II. CREATION

The monotheistic concept of divine uniqueness has an advantage over the pantheistic concept of divine unity: it immediately defines God's relation to nature and man. For the monotheist no longer considers nature an enigma, to be solved only by the assumption that God Himself is hypostatized in, and therefore absolutely identical with the physical world. Such an assumption, as made by pantheism, represents merely a reaction to the perplexing and incomprehensible existence of nature which would seem to be nothing but an accident, unless it were understood as a hypostatization of God.

The new idea of the uniquely One God, however, saves man

from this desperate thought. When the physical world is no longer regarded as a puzzling accident, man does not need a concept of God that would eliminate all distinction between deity and nature. Instead, the uniqueness of God's being provides the explanation and the ground for nature's being.

Just as the idea of being as such proves a useful premise for the scientific exploration of becoming, so does the idea of the uniqueness of divine being prove to be a necessary as well as productive premise for solving the problem of the being of nature and of man.

It is an essential corollary of the One-God concept that nature and man be brought into existence. God and nature are not co-equal let alone identical powers. The existence of nature is rather a conceptual consequence of God's uniqueness. Creation is a necessary attribute of God.

Hence, neither creation nor God's unique Oneness are notions incompatible with human reason. Nor does creation—an absolutely rational concept within the logic of being—constitute a mystery that can be rendered intelligible only by a religious but not by an ordinary scientific mode of cognition. Just as God's unique Oneness is consonant with the logical concept of substance, so is creation consonant with the ontological concept of the uniquely One God.

Accordingly, Jewish religious teaching has, by and large, approached the concept of creation in this rational spirit. Indeed, even the first word of the story of creation with which the Bible opens was already interpreted to mean not merely a "beginning" but a state of "primacy." The notion of "beginning" is still part of the conceptual world of cosmogony.

Yet even the words "creation in the beginning" were not considered wholly adequate to convey the real meaning of the concept of divine creation. They were therefore augmented by the term "renewal of the world." And to the daily prayer was added the sentence: "Who in His goodness renews, every day continually, the work of the beginning."

Thus, continuous renewal of the world becomes the central idea, while the notion of its creation in the beginning loses significance. Every day represents a new beginning. The mystery of the world's beginning is thus transmuted into the everyday wonder of its renewal, that is, its maintenance. The creator becomes the sustainer, and God's uniqueness becomes manifest as divine providence.

This transformation signifies a tremendous change in religious thinking, a change that sets religion apart from mythology and imbues it with true originality.

Now the problem is no longer creation out of nothingness nor even out of primordial matter. The notion of nothingness has vanished; it has been absorbed by the comprehensive concept of God's singular, unique being. Thus, nothingness is no longer a specter haunting man's cognitive faculty: God's Oneness has become the source and ground of nature's existence. . . .

As we said, creation means renewal and as such a constantly ongoing work which logic refers to as continuity. Religious thinking does not stop at this logical interpretation, however; the notion of renewal soon comes to denote providence. But with the concept of providence, the logical meaning of the God-idea is transmuted into an ethical meaning; and it is here that the real elemental force of the One-God concept fully unfolds.

Mythical man is interested only in the question of the world's "where-from?" With the development of religion, this question recedes into the background, dislodged by a new one: "Where-to?" The world's cause and its primal ground no longer pose the main and all-consuming epistemological problem; now the question about the purpose of nature and especially about the purpose of man takes up a center position in man's quest for knowledge.

Monotheism leads to the insight that it is the One God who, uniquely and providentially sustaining nature as well as man, gives purpose to both. Without such a purpose, the world would be devoid of meaning.

Or can it be considered meaningful when pantheism decrees, as it has done at all times, that God and world are identical? Can this notion of identity of God and nature bestow any real meaning even on the latter? It obviously can do no such thing, just as it cannot impart any true significance to divine being.

Nature gains significance not by its alleged identity with God but by God's providence. And the true significance of the One

God, in turn, is enhanced by this significance of nature. Yet the mythological mode of cognition, still characteristic of much of theological thinking, persists in its logical inquiry, the question of the world's "where-from?" There, creation remains an act of divine omnipotence. But with the emerging notion of the world's day-by-day renewal through which the concept of creation is transformed into that of providence, theology turns into teleology, the goal-oriented mode of perception.

This goal-awareness gives rise to ethics and establishes a special field within general logic, a new area of particular human concerns. Here, the emphasis is on the proper study of man's mind and nature and of their manifestations throughout history.

One can easily see why Spinoza, the founder of a latter-day pantheism, wishes to eliminate any teleological thinking from the arsenal of cognitive concepts, and why he refers to teleology as "the asylum of ignorance." His concern is exclusively with the necessity of the laws of nature, that is, with causality. And because of the existence of these laws, he recognizes no mode of being other than that of nature. And nature, as pointed out repeatedly, is assumed to be identical with God.

But how can one construct an ethics once one has declared teleological concepts null and void?

It is not the least of the many ambiguities afflicting Spinoza's system—beginning with his *Definitions*—that he refers to his metaphysics and its addendum of a psychology of the emotions not simply by this descriptive term but, instead, calls his book *Ethics*. The necessity of natural laws, his guiding principle, is supposed to point the way to an ethics! Necessity, he asserts, is the only purpose there is; to assume any other would merely lead us deeper into ignorance. Nature itself is God, with necessity their common ground. And man is merely a human manifestation of nature, with no purpose other than that determined by necessity. Nor has God any being other than that circumscribed by the necessity of natural laws. There is no creation of nature by God because there is no providence for nature in God. Nor is God the uniquely One. Instead, the concept of unity is here disclosed in all its dangerousness: unity becomes union, a merging of nature and God, who, subsequently, is not the uniquely One God but merely the one substance.

Substance is a fundamental concept of logic and science. Here, however, it becomes a fundamental concept of ethics as well, an ethics which considers man solely under the aspect of nature, subject to its laws of necessity and with no higher purpose. But if purpose is declared null and void, so is ethics, and the use of this word for the title of his book makes Spinoza guilty of an act of usurpation.

Spinoza destroyed the concept of God's uniqueness by identifying Him with nature. Yet by doing so, he made it eminently clear that the concept of uniqueness is indeed superior to that of unity.

III. REVELATION

If creation is not to be regarded as a mystery, revelation must not be seen as such either. Nor should these two notions be considered as irreconcilable with the sharply defined and clear concept of God's unique being, but rather as its corollaries.

For God's uniqueness not only constitutes the ground of the world's existence; it is also indispensable for the concept of man (insofar as he, a being endowed with reason, is distinct from the rest of creation).

But reason is not merely a faculty of man's theoretical intellect. It is responsible for his sense of morality; that is, it must shape as well as sustain man's moral intellect.

Revelation must proceed from the One and Only God as the wellspring of the one and only morality for all mankind.

The rationality of Jewish theology is already evident in the circumscriptive definition of revelation as "revelation at Sinai." This literary fact alone makes one wonder: after all, is not the entire Torah revealed teaching? Why then should the designation "revelation" be limited solely to the Decalogue?

The Decalogue constitutes the basis of all humane ethics insofar as this is grounded in the One, imageless, and incorporeal God.

And this ethics has as far-reaching an effect on man's innermost being, on his wishes and desires, as on the social structure of his body politic. Therefore the Sabbath, with its liberation of slave and hireling from uninterrupted labor, occupies the very center of this quintessence of moral precepts.

Moreover, the Bible refers to the revelation at Sinai by a term that would seem to reject, with naive determination, any semblance between this event and a mysterious disclosure or unveiling: the "Giving of the Torah" (*Mattan Torah*). That means that the Jewish genius for language emphasizes here not the object given, the gift, but exclusively the act of giving, that is, communication. And this communication signifies God's giving of Himself, as indeed He gives of Himself in everything that issues from Him. The religious spirit of monotheism does not speculate about the mode of this issuance. It does, though, assiduously try to keep the idea of the One God's communication to man free from any material element.

God creates man's spirit. He creates this spirit of man as the holy spirit, the spirit of holiness.[3] And inherent in this creation is the very solution of what one might feel inclined to regard as the mystery of God's communication to man.

The Mosaic religion represents not merely theoretical teachings, however; it is also an account of Israel's history. From the very first, the people had to be reminded of its history and origin in the hope of impressing upon the national consciousness its spiritual task and of affecting a realization of this task through a heightened national self-awareness and a deepened national enthusiasm.

The apogee of Israel's spiritual history is represented by the luminary figure of Moses. To be sure, he was never considered a hero or a demigod, let alone a divine mediator. Nevertheless, it was inevitable that he was the one to transmit the revelation to the people; that is, it was he who brought down the tablets of the Decalogue. For it took such a luminary to pierce the mythological darkness and infuse the people with that sense of history which would enable them to comprehend the spirituality of the One God.

It is characteristic that Moses lives on in Jewish consciousness

3. See "The Holy Spirit."

as "our teacher Moses." In no way is he our revealer; he is simply our teacher. And what he transmits from God to people is thought of as "the teaching." For all transmission of spiritual values is teaching.

Yet it is quite consistent with the primitive tenor of the Biblical story that Moses' exceptional status is described by metaphors that border on the non-spiritual. Thus, the Bible does not hesitate to say that God spoke to Moses "from mouth to mouth." But God can no more speak to the mouth of Moses than He himself can have a mouth. Ibn Ezra, in his clear-cut language, interprets this metaphor correctly as meaning "without intermediary." By this single explanation, the entire problem of communication is elucidated and solved.

Nevertheless, the Biblical account goes on to say in its naiveté: "The Lord spoke with you face to face in the mount out of the midst of the fire" (Deuteronomy 5:4). That is, God has also spoken to the entire people from face to face, hence from mouth to mouth. Thus, Moses' exceptional status is rendered void for he now shares it with the entire people. And this appeal to the people itself—the fact, that is, that the people is to receive the revelation on an equal footing with Moses—does much to bring about that sense of peoplehood which must be aroused if Israel is to understand its mission.

Yet there still remains a suspicion that the event at Sinai implies a materialization of divine spirituality. But this suspicion is laid to rest in Deuteronomy. For here, the process of national self-spiritualization is summed up in a formulation that amounts to a literary miracle. It says: "The Lord made not this covenant with our fathers, but with us, even us, who are all of us here alive this day" (Deuteronomy 5:3). With this repeated use of the small word "us," the stage of revelation is transposed from the past right into the present.

And this prepares the way for the emergence of that great concept of Deuteronomy which completely internalizes the Torah's origin by placing it solely and exclusively in man himself. The alleged mystery of revelation is simply and definitively solved by that oratory in the fields of Moab which I do not hesitate to call the most grandiose work of art in the entire history of rhetoric: "For this commandment which I command thee this day, it is not too hard for thee, neither is it far off. It is not in heaven that thou shouldst say: 'Who shall go up for us to heaven, and bring it unto us?' . . . But the word is very nigh unto thee, in thy mouth, and in thy heart, that thou mayest do it" (Deuteronomy 30:11–14).

This removes the last shadow of doubt one may have harbored with regard to the pure spirituality of revelation. The teaching is not in heaven but in man's mouth, in his faculty of speech and in his heart, and therefore also in his mind. It did not come to man from without; it originated within him. It is rooted in his spirit which God, the uniquely One, has put into man as the holy spirit, the spirit of holiness. And that is the spirit of morality.

Now, does revelation still appear to be a mystery? Is it not rather a necessary corollary of the concept of the One God?

The One and Only God alone can reveal the one and only morality. Morality therefore is indivisible. It must be one and the same for all nations and throughout all times. Representing an element of the eternal and the holy in the human heart, morality must forever remain distinct from and independent of all temporary changes in man's ethical orientation.

The assertion that this holy moral law originated in man himself in no way contradicts the concept of divine revelation. In fact, to say that this law flowed from man's heart and mind is to say that it was revealed by God. For it was God who imbued man with spirit. "He formed the spirit of man within him" (Zechariah 12:1). Therefore the holy spirit, the spirit of holiness, is man's most essential and inalienable property of which even his sin cannot divest him.

And just as scientific philosophy defines a primary and eternal principle as an a priori concept—in contradistinction to the changing notions of psychology—so revelation must be distinguished in its a priori significance from all other phenomena throughout the history of religion.

Revelation is that which is eternal—and as such divine—in the spirit of mankind.

CHAPTER 3

Prophetic Ideals

Editor's Note

Even during and after the Exile, Israel remains God's inheritance. Yet Israel's concept of its chosenness is, Cohen is convinced, not a mark of Jewish arrogance. It is "a battle-cry for divine justice" and a challenge to live an exemplary life. Moreover, Jewish chosenness represents "history's means to accomplish the divine chosenness of mankind." For Judaism must become a world religion if the prophetic ideal of one mankind, united in justice and universal peace, is to become a historical reality.

This reality—and for Cohen, all "reality means realization"—is the final goal of Messianism, a manifestation of that ultimate perfection of human life to which prophetic Judaism aspires and for which it hopes. The prophetic, the truly mature image of the Messiah is therefore not that of a man but of a time, an "end of days" when "the real day will dawn: the day of mankind, the day of morality, the day of the moral individual."

The prophets are neither mythologists nor theologians; they are not caught in the web of mythic and mystic tales ancient nations spin. They are, in fact, not even interested in their people's past; nor do they engage in idle speculation about things which are beyond human understanding. Their concern is with man's here and now and with his future—that is, with his present ethical conduct and his future moral development. For the prophets believe in a future when man's highest human potential will be actualized, a belief Cohen considers of central importance to or even a necessary postulate of all religious faith "and indeed its most wondrous flower."

The prophets' idea of God as the righteous, just, and loving Creator of the world leads them to set up an ideal for man's righteous, just, and loving deed in this world. Though fully aware of

105

man's shortcomings, they are convinced of his moral perfectibility. Cohen shares this attitude and, with a certain wistfulness, even suggests that the Tower of Babel, the Biblical symbol of men's divisiveness, might one day be transformed into a lighthouse which will illumine men's minds with a clear understanding of their common humanity.

The Style of the Prophets

The style of the prophets, unique to the Israelite people, has become a timeless literary possession of all mankind. The substance of prophetic rhetoric is morality. Morality is Plato's main concern too. But Plato wishes to make the science of morality autonomous and, in spite of his fondness for the old myths, independent of religion. His dialogue therefore becomes a dialectic which creates and structures moral concepts in the context of a scientific system. Hence his disdain for the poetry of rhetoric, whose charms, though, he could not wholly resist, as evidenced by his retention of many myths.

The prophets, on the other hand, consider themselves to be above the web of myths their people had spun. They rarely refer to even the most sublime moments of their nation's early existence, on the assumption that the national past will eventually be forgotten. But though they may neglect the past, they use their rich poetic endowment to depict the future and thus, in their rhetoric, prove to be genuine and great poets. The prophetic style is not merely a matter of aesthetics; it brings into focus the problem of the relationship between morality and religion, while Plato's style points up the relationship of ethics and religion. Ethics is the science of morality and as such not the concern of the prophets. They are artists, not philosophers. A consideration of their style seems therefore particularly significant. For instance, does the fact that their art gives rise to moral ideas in any way mean that these ideas are merely figments of the imagination, sick products of some divine madness? Or should we ascribe truth to them, though they lack scientific grounding?

The fate of religion hinges on this question. Religion is not science; subsequently, it can also not be ethics. But does this make its morality a mere artifact? Are the prophets nothing but artists, and is their style merely an exercise in aesthetics? Or could it be that this style of theirs creates a certain border area, a zone between art and science which constitutes religion? True, religion comprises also the realm of myths. But the prophets fight against these myths, as even Plato felt compelled to do. And by their very opposition to mythology the prophets create a new kind of religion. The new religion of the One God is the work of art created by and expressive of their particular style. In fact, the prophets would not have a style of their own if their religion were approximately the same as the mythology of other nations. As it is, the style of the prophets—who, though neither philosophers nor merely artists, are most creative teachers—expresses the special character of religion in contradistinction to mythology, art, or science.

Monotheistic religion is the teaching of God as the One and Only. The concept of divine Oneness, distinguishing religion from myth, serves as a symbol for the abstract notion that there is a fundamental difference between God and everything that is not God. God's unique Oneness sets His being and essence apart from all other being.[1]

But what does this symbol mean to the prophets? They are no theologians, after all. God's teaching is to them exclusively moral teaching. God must therefore also imply a relation to all those modes of being distinct from His own nature. In fact, all morality is predicated on such a relation. And it is such a relation, too, which is meant by the term transcendence. God is not nature; yet His unique Oneness and transcendence imply His relation to nature. God is not man; yet He would not be the One and Only if His relation to man did not inhere in Him. And it is this relation of God to man and hence also to nature which is the concern of

1. See "Uniqueness Rather Than Unity of God."

prophetic morality. Actually, it is not even correct to speak of a relation between God and man because God and man are not equal members of a relation. By Himself, God is not a relational concept. He is the very ground and premise on which man, by himself, must predicate and sustain all relationships. Without God, there would be no man, no man, that is, as moral being.

Thus, God becomes the Father of man. The animal too is God's creature. But man is, as it were, His creature in a twofold sense, for God is also the originator of man's morality. God's mercy extends to all His creatures; but His fatherhood is a concept that characterizes His relationship to man alone. "Therefore doth He instruct sinners in the [right] way" (Psalms 25:8). If Judaism rejected the plastic arts, it certainly did not neglect the art of poetry. As Father of man, God is seen as the God of love. And the entire poetry of love, in all its aspects and motifs, is poured out in the prophets' descriptions of their God. He is bridegroom and husband, father and comforting mother. He is the shepherd clasping His lambs to His bosom. He is friend, teacher, and mentor. Always and everywhere, it is God who constitutes the ground and precondition for all man's relations. But He Himself must never become man. If He did, the ground of all relations would cease to be; instead, there would be identity, the identity of divine and human nature. And that is contrary to the style of the prophets: "For not a man is God; God am I, not man." [2]

God's Oneness also implies His relation to nature. God is not nature or else He could not stand in any relation to it. Moreover, an equation of God with nature would make any differentiation between good and evil meaningless inasmuch as nature is neither good nor evil. But since the God of the prophets is the Creator of nature, nature becomes the symbol of morality. There is, however, a characteristic difference in the way the rhetoric of the prophets and the poetry of the Psalms speak about nature. In the Book of Psalms, nature, in its awesomeness as well as its loveliness, symbolizes the divine Creator. The sun, the lodestar of nature, goes forth like a bridegroom from his tent, joyful as a young hero, to run his course. But the prophet will not tolerate such a glorifica-

2. Probably a reference to and adaptation of Numbers 23:19.

tion of nature: "The moon should blush, and the sun be ashamed" (Isaiah 24:23).[3] Nature, along with man—as a natural being— must be downgraded. "And man is bowed down, and man is humbled, and the eyes of the lofty are humbled" (Isaiah 5:15). . . .

The fact that nature and man are wholly set apart from God adds a tragic note to the prophets' style. For it is the core-meaning of tragedy that man, by himself, is not equal to his ethical task and endowment. This disparity constitutes a pathological element in man's nature: he is born to be moral, yet he fashions for himself a god of clay and wood and says to the wood: "you are my god." His intellectual creativity and artistic imagination become his downfall. And not only his intellect drives him to his own ruin but his inadequate sense of morality too; thus, love becomes lewdness.

God has chosen Israel for His wife. But as the people proves faithless to the covenant of its youth, Israel becomes a whore. Here, the prophets' tragic style turns into satire. And who knows whether that dreadful castigation of his contemporaries' sexual licentiousness, preserved in the memory of history, is not the product of some satirist's imagination rather than a historian's description of the mores of his time?

As mentioned before, the prophets conceive of God as the very ground of all morality and its premise, and as the foundation on which all relations of man as a natural and moral being are based. But as natural being, man represents two modes of existence: that of an individual and that of a tribe or nation. The prophets do not start out with the individual in order to determine man's relation to God. For them, man means nation or rather nations. They do not even regard their own people as representative of the concept man but instead those nations or states with which their country establishes a more or less close contact. Politics is the native soil of prophetic religion. Thus, their moral teachings have topical overtones; voiced within wide practical contexts, they open important perspectives and give rise to basic questions of morality.

By referring repeatedly to Israel's Canaanitic origins, the

3. The J.P.S. translation reads: "Then the moon shall be confounded, and the sun ashamed."

prophets introduce a concept that combines both national and supranational views. Ezekiel does so ironically, as a means of castigating Israel for its apostasy: "Behold, everyone that uses proverbs shall use this proverb against thee, saying: as the mother, so her daughter . . . your mother was a Hittite, and your father an Amorite. And thine elder sister is Samaria, and thine younger sister . . . is Sodom" (Ezekiel 16:44 ff.). There is no irony whatever in Amos, however, when he reproaches Phoenicia and Egypt for forgetting their "brotherly covenant" with Judah. In this way, a naive pan-semitism helps to demolish national conceit and arrogance, and prepares the way for the universalism of mankind.

To the prophet, nations are representative of man as natural being; even his own dearly beloved people is nothing but such a natural organism above which there hovers, as yet inchoate, the spirit of God. This spirit will have to be formed and developed: it will have to become the spirit of the One, the new God, if out of the many nations one mankind is to be born.

Mankind is the archetypal, the fundamental Gestalt [4] envisaged by moral man. Yet, how far removed are the nations from this ideal of mankind! Should one not despair of their moral perfectibility? The style of the prophets avoids such pessimism; at first, however, it does not sound a note of optimism either but speaks instead in terms of a tragic pathos. War, that political expression of envy and jealousy, marks the historical cycle of any nation's existence. But any war a nation wages against its neighbors will soon rage within its own borders. Thus, the prophets' awesome imagination depicts all of war's horrors. The misfortunes of battle constitute the incessantly repeated theme of their epic satire. They are almost excessively inventive in their description of every detail of the desolation, destruction, misery, and dehumanization wars not only will but actually should bring upon the nations. Their wantonness will cause their downfall. The people claim to be heroes and wish to be celebrated as such and to be glorified in songs. Debauched and cruel, they desire to give vent to their self-conceit; but their lustful drives will ruin them. Once again, we

4. German for "shape," "form"; a morphological configuration or structure.

see a tragic trend in man's nature as, in an excess of self-importance, he seems to exclaim: "I, and nothing besides me."

But though the contrast between man's aspirations and his actual achievements constitute a tragic motif, there must be some positive element hidden even in his downfall. For who is it that causes the mighty to fall? Once again, it is none other than the One God. The horror of war cannot possibly be an end in itself. Horses and chariots, spears and swords, towers and walls, killings and desecrations—all must serve a higher purpose. In fact, all of nature must serve this purpose. Mountains and rivers, the trees of the forest and the cedars of Lebanon, winds and seasons, heaven and earth—all turn into instruments of war. Habakkuk once asks: "Is it that thine anger is kindled against the rivers?" (Habakkuk 3:8). This question discloses a profound uneasiness: is it really permissible to think of nature as God's whiplash, and may the terrors of nature really be made into objects of religious poetry?

Horror is certainly not an aesthetic end in itself. Nature, the work of God, is also His working tool and as such serves the horrors of war. It is God who uses war to demolish the nations' titanic arrogance. The Tower of Babel must become a lighthouse and illuminate the political history of the nations. Building the tower created confusion among the people and made of human beings separate nations. If therefore these nations are to be transfigured into one mankind, they must slough off their unhistoric existence. Out of war's desolation, they must arise to new life. War represents their natural existence; but this must come to an end if a new life, a life of morality, is to emerge.

When He brings war to the nations as well as to Israel, God is the God of justice. Justice is one of the two pivotal attributes of God's nature. And it is characteristic that the Hebrew term for the one intrinsically also denotes the other: for complementing divine justice is divine love, and the Hebrew *tsedakah* means justice as well as love. It is therefore easy to see why still another term [5] is needed to describe that aspect of justice which is wholly distinguished from love. Yet this word, commonly rendered as "retalia-

5. *G'mul,* "retribution," "retaliation," "reward," "recompense" (from root *gamal;* see, for instance, I Samuel 24:18; Isaiah 3:9 *et al*).

tion," has a sinister connotation, and in this sense is clearly inapplicable to the God of our prophets. Divine retaliation must be understood to mean God's just retribution. And as divine justice conceptually implies love, so does divine retribution linguistically imply consolation.

Depicting God's retributive judgment as a disclosure of His justice, the prophetic style, marked by severity and harshness, occasionally reaches a ferocious crescendo. In such passages the artist gets the better of the religious thinker. This trend, however, represents merely a collateral line in the prophets' rhetoric, and contrasts sharply with another line which runs much broader and deeper. In Isaiah, especially, the dominant trend is one of consolation. Here, the horrors described are more those of nature than of war. Earthquakes, floods, storm and hail, tumbling rocks and uprooted trees—nature's symbols of war wreaking havoc on the land and ravaging it—they are here predominantly signs and portents of divine retribution. But these horrors indicate exceptional states of nature. More often, nature heralds peace. And the individual who is genuinely in tune with nature will find peace there. Thus, Jeremiah brings consolation or, as the Talmud says, he is all consolation. As war means revenge, so peace means consolation. And Isaiah is the prophet of peace, of the true peace of God.

But while wars shockingly reveal the primitive nature of nations, peace will transform them into moral mankind. To transform nations into mankind must therefore be the primary postulate of any ethics. Yet Plato does not recognize this relation between nation and mankind. And since he fails even to pose this ultimate problem, his scientific ethics must of course fail to solve it. This then constitutes the triumph of the prophets' religion over the philosophy of ethics: the prophets, and they alone, discovered the idea of mankind. Moreover, this fundamental principle of Judaism has marvellously proven its methodological soundness. For the concept of the One God is the prerequisite for the relation of nation and mankind, and it was prophetic religion alone which conceived of this relation. Verily, "Have we not all one father, hath not one God created us?" (Malachi 2:10).

Along with peace, which will make all nations into one mankind, the prophet emphasizes the attribute of love. An attribute of **God** must, as such, become an attribute of man, as moral man. **Man** does not serve as archetype of God, though this might be said of the gods of Greece whom her poets seem to have invented. But it is different with our God who, as the One, the spiritual God is no mirror-image of man. God's love means love of mankind, that love through which mankind comes into being and without which it cannot exist. And it is this divine love which guarantees that the envisioned mankind will become a reality.

Discovering the true meaning of God's love, the prophet becomes the great poet of the love of mankind. Moreover, love, as divine attribute, is now regarded as the principal characteristic of divine nature. To know God therefore means to love Him. Love is God's very essence. It is also a basic affect of the prophet's emotions and therefore becomes a basic motif of their style.

Visions of a time that will bring peace to the world lead to an awareness of temporal distance. The notion of "the end of days," of a "then" dominates every "now" and all reality. So far, man has not lived up to the prophet's world-historical goals. Instead, nations have been attacking each other like wild beasts, thinking themselves noble warriors and heroes. But now "the end of days" must be understood to mean the end of all days which are not God's days.

But the prophets, who from Amos on have proclaimed peace as a universal, world-historical goal, are more than merely epic poets of a world-historical future. True, these prophetic visions have the magic charm of a cosmological epos; but this analogy tends to obscure the immediate involvement of the prophets' hearts and minds in mankind's destiny, that favorite idea of theirs. Though the prophets' every utterance is indeed permeated by sheer lyricism, the idea of the Messianic age with its universal peace neither is nor remains merely lyrical abstraction. For as the prophet himself—indeed, *qua* himself—fondly nurtures the idea of a Messianic mankind in his heart, this idea becomes the lyrical emotion of love.

Lyric poetry is primarily a poetry of nature. This holds true for the style of the prophets too. Lyrically depicting the peace that love brings to the world of nature, they symbolize the peace that love will bring to the world of man. Thus, when their love of man and their new sense of history will have raised the nations to the level of a united mankind, the earth will be God's "holy mountain," and there will be an end to the nations' iniquity.

This is what the prophets ask and what they hope for the rebirth of mankind. They do not, however, say that this also represents the attainment of all moral goals for the individual, for man as such. Here, the prophets' main concern is the disparity between the people's narrow nationalism and their own vision of mankind. To realize this vision is to understand the will of God. In this sense, knowledge of God will lead to universal peace, within historical time. And in this sense, it will indeed be true that God has made heaven and earth, and that He will be acknowledged and proclaimed as the Lord and God of all the earth and of the entire world whose very ends He has created. And in the face of all the skepticism the prophets, as dreamers of distant days, encountered, they boldly proclaimed: "Behold, I make a new heaven, and a new earth" (Isaiah 65:17).[6] The new heaven is the new morality; and the new earth, a new mankind.

One might assume that the lyricism of such poetry of eternal peace and of men's love for one another would make a perfect idyl. The style of the prophets, however, does not achieve such final tranquility. Their lyric poetry reflects the tragic conflicts which had originally caused them to develop and extol the idea of one mankind. Having first been called on the world-stage by high politics with all its complex problems, its questions about fights with neighboring nations, and its need to decide what alliances were desirable and what capitulations inevitable, the prophets are fervent patriots. . . . Envisaging the destruction of the entire nation, they proclaim that a remnant of Israel will survive. And their hope rests with this remnant, this new root and holy seed. For though heaven and earth may vanish, though mountains may sway and sun and moon may alter their course, Israel's name and seed will be perpetuated.

6. This is a translation of Cohen's rendition of the text.

There can be no doubt: even Israel's sins cannot lead to its complete ruin. Not only the prophets' fervent patriotism but their very Messianism protects them from contemplating such a possibility. For even the enemy nations have their Messianic "end of days," and will experience a reprieve from their imprisonment and a return to their country. More than that: they will be united with Israel. They too will ascend the holy mountain and will rejoice in the Temple of the One God. The concept of a unification of all nations into one mankind, under Israel's religious guidance, indubitably represents the highest triumph as well as the most profound substance of prophetic patriotism. And yet this concept too is inherently painful and tragic.

The prophetic pronouncements are subject to frequent changes in mood, changing abruptly from threats of punishment to sudden consolations. One cannot help but feel that the prophets are conscious of and tortured by some inner contradiction: Israel will be saved; that is, it will survive as a nation. In fact, even the pagan peoples will be saved from destruction, or else the prophet would forever have to weep for Edom and bemoan Moab. All nations will go up to Jerusalem and all will find their true home there. But how shall Jerusalem, this one city, be able to absorb the entire world population? Is it therefore not an inevitable and irrefutable conclusion that Jerusalem, once it has become a moral concept of the new world history as well as the hub of the earth, must cease to be a political concept? Here, a new tragic concept emerges: the prophet must lose his country, for mankind will become his country. "Weep not for the dead, neither bemoan him; but weep sore for him that goeth away, for he shall return no more, nor see his native country" (Jeremiah 22:10). That is the melancholy note which sounds in any jubilation regarding the prophetic vision of the future.

Israel remains God's inheritance; but now Egypt too is called "My people and Assyria the work of My hands" (Isaiah 19:25). This trend already starts with Amos, who equates Israel with Ethiopia, and it is the drop of bitterness mixed into every joyous cup of the prophets' patriotism. Even the concept of chosenness originates in this insight: "You only have I known of all the families of the earth; therefore I will visit upon you all your iniquities" (Amos 3:2).

Thus, chosenness is not a mark of arrogance; it is the battle cry for divine justice. Chosenness means Israel's vocation to proclaim the One God as the redeemer of mankind. But even in those passages which express, in no uncertain and quite uninhibited terms, Israel's sense of exhilaration over its vocation, a slight tremor of melancholy can be felt, however softly or secretly. It accompanies the inescapable conclusion that Israel must sacrifice its peoplehood for its God. Its name and seed will be saved but its state must disappear. A nation is transformed into a community (*Gemeinde*), and it is the community alone which will survive. The community of Israel replaces the people of the covenant. For now there is a new covenant, written into the heart and intended to make the earlier one sink into oblivion. We are indebted for this exposition to that specific patriot among the prophets, that lyricist of patriotism, Jeremiah. His insight is the source of all emotions underlying every prophetic oration, satire as well as idyl. And the lament about the inner necessity of our wanderings, to the end of days, has remained the leitmotif of Jewish existence. This kind of sentiment distinguishes the style of the prophets from the poetry of all other peoples. It is the note of human suffering sounded even in moments of sublime human joy.

The Talmud offers a fine stylistic observation. Rabbi Johanan says that wherever the Bible mentions God's greatness, it also praises His humility. The Hebrew term [7] has the same root as the word for poverty. The poor man is a living contradiction of the concept of human equality, the equality of God's children. The prophets' work for moral reform centers on the idea of the Sabbath which becomes the symbol of social morality. And as the rainbow is the symbol of peace in the sky, so the Sabbath is the symbol of peace on earth. Human beings are not meant to be divided into free men and laborers. All men are equal, for all have been called

---

7. The Hebrew terms *anavah*, "humility" (see, for instance, Psalm 18:38) and *aniyut*, "poverty" (see, for instance, Exodus 22:24) have the same root.

upon to lead a moral life. But the prerequisite for morality is knowledge, and knowledge means, first and foremost, knowledge of God. Obedience and undertanding are the same, in the language of the prophets. By stressing the need for listening [that is, obedience] rather than offering sacrifices, a practice they oppose, the prophets make individually practiced morality the basis of all religion. There must be no division between priests and laymen: "Ye shall be unto Me a kingdom of priests, and a holy nation" (Exodus 19:6).

The premise that any individual is capable of acquiring knowledge and understanding is indispensable for the notion that all men can participate in a moral civilization. And this notion constitutes the substance of the prophets' social ethics. It is interesting to note, in passing, that the socialist point of view is represented with political and juridical determination not so much by the cosmopolitan Isaiah as by the patriotic Jeremiah. For the latter, knowledge of God and social justice are virtually the same. And it is his concept of social justice that motivates him to advocate the sanctification of the Sabbath, particularly with regard to the laborer, that traditional bearer of burdens: "Take heed for the sake of your souls, and bear no burden on the sabbath day, nor bring it in by the gates of Jerusalem" (Jeremiah 17:21).

Justice and love are equal components of the prophetic style. Isaiah knows no higher praise even for the Messiah than to say that he will judge the poor with justice, and that justice is the girdle of his loins. "Then justice shall dwell in the wilderness, and righteousness shall abide in the fruitful field" (Isaiah 32:16). The Messiah will clothe himself in justice as in an armor, and all the people will be righteous. It is as if the prophet meant to say: everyone, or no one. For this reason, he considers himself a prophet of poverty quite as much as a prophet of the nations. Here, the style of the prophet is double-edged. He lashes out against the rich who oppress the poor, and against princes, priests, and prophets who glibly cry "peace, peace" when there is no peace.

The social viewpoint from which the prophets regard public life influences their style in yet another characteristic way. Neither turning sentimental when describing the misery of the poor nor yet

going so far as to extol the poor man's blessedness, they do not
dwell much on pity or on mercy. They are adamant, however, in
demanding that the poor be given their rights. But wherever these
rights are denied the poor, the prophetic anger is turned not merely
against the incumbent rulers but equally against the means society
employs to gloss over its own mendacity. And foremost among
these means is art. Catering to luxury and emphasizing only the
beautiful, it denies the fact that wretchedness and destitution have
a tight grip on the poor. This is the reason why the prophetic zeal
is turned against art, and not merely against the luxury of women
or the pretentiousness of the rich. The prophets do not only attack the weakening of public morals or the alliance with idol worship into which art—sculpture and music alike—has entered. They
do not disdain architecture or music as long as these serve to
enhance Temple worship. But they are deeply suspicious of that
one-sided attitude of an aesthetics which is unconcerned with all
moral problems of civilization, and regards them as something that
has to be borne with realistic equanimity if one wishes to enjoy
rather than give up the golden apples from the tree of art, which it
considers the real tree of life. It is this delusion of a one-sided
sense of aesthetics which the prophets decry, and their rebuke is
therefore directed quite as much against a sentimental reverie of
nature as against art. . . .

Beautiful nature must also perish; so must all works of art as
well as all men. Trees and men share a common fate—they sink
into the ground. . . . As a symbol the Messiah, who will bring
a better future, is himself an aesthetic figure. In spite of his inner
power, he is a poor man who is depicted with the warmth or the
fire of empathy. He rides not a splendid horse but a donkey, and
allows himself to be led to the slaughter like a lamb. Though he
will judge the nations by the rod of his mouth, he is destitute,
without beauty, and lacks all the charms of a hero; yet God's spirit
emanates from him.

It is both the spirituality of morality and moral idealism which
expose and oppose aesthetic narrowness and narrow-mindedness
and make common cause with all who reject sculptured gods and
heroes. The Messiah is no hero but the "servant of the Lord." His

attributes are not strength and beauty but illness and suffering. Compassion and pity for the poor of the earth are poured into this portrayal of the servant of the Lord. But here too a strong and tragic motif prevents empty laments. The Messiah is the herald of mankind. He will end all social misery. The poetry of social compassion points, with all the magic of hope, towards the future. The present, however, with its unfilled needs, unnatural oppression, glaring injustices, vain conceits, and bragging untruths deserves no pity. It asks for bitter, hard, truthful satire to rip the aesthetic veil from man's work of deception.

If one word could characterize the morality of the prophets, that word would be "truth." The prophets criticize nothing quite as much as conceit and lies which they relentlessly pursue into all their hiding places. For them, truth is the very ground of the individual's existence. Truth is veracity of being.

Therefore the prophets' zeal is turned against the hypocrisy of Israel's worship. They are aroused not only by the people's defection to the ranks of idolaters but by the sham of the public sacrificial cult. They ask for the service of the heart and mind, the service of truthfulness. . . .

The prophet envisions the end of days; for then the real day will dawn: the day of mankind, the day of morality, the day of the moral individual. . . .

On Messianism

The Jewish God-concept reaches its ultimate perfection in the Messianic idea. This idea grew out of an historical development, as all ideas do. It is, however, the way in which an idea makes use of any given historical motives that determines its true originality. The prophets would probably not have conceived the idea of a Messiah had the political history of their people not suggested such a possibility to them. But did it ever occur to any other nation to hope, in the midst of its political decline, for its restoration in some far-away future? In addition, the prophets proclaimed the reestablishment of their state not after but long before its fall—and as a postulate of divine justice at that. Hence, political motives played but an incidental role in the emergence of this autonomous thought.

Moreover, and this is the main point, the prophets did not make the renascence of their own state the single or even primary subject of their public pronouncements. On the contrary, they announced the eventual restoration also of those states and nations which had fought against their own people. Faced with the events of the past, they conceived the notion of a future. As an historical concept of time, this notion constitutes the true significance and real discovery of their Messianic thinking.

True, there is also an empirical element that motivates and provides a topical starting point for their thinking. The king was anointed in Israel. And David was that glorious king who had established not only the state but, in a real sense, also the Temple where his psalms were now chanted as prayers. Just as the prophets' vision of a future is naturally tied to the restoration of their own people, whose destruction their sense of religious justice had demanded, so does their hope for the future cling to this ideal royal figure. Thus, the Messiah becomes the scion of the house of David, one who is anointed, who is like a king. But soon this image changes. The anointed one, no longer a king, is transfigured into the symbol of human suffering. True hope can emanate from this symbolic figure alone, and in it alone can mankind see a true warrant for its restoration.

It is only now that the full meaning of the Messianic idea unfolds in all its grandeur. The prophets' concern is not merely with their own people. "It is too light a thing that thou shouldest be my servant to raise up the tribes of Jacob . . . I will also give thee for a light of the nations": thus Deutero-Isaiah (49:6), in spite of his patriotic grief, characterizes Israel's universal task. All prophets, even those prior to the Exile, think of the Messiah in such universalistic terms. They see him as the symbol of universal peace, when all mankind will gather around as one flock to worship the One God. As a prerequisite, though, men must advance the cause of morality on earth; most of all, they must make wars disappear and prepare the way for a future in which life can be lived in harmony and justice. . . .

Here, it is actually difficult to distinguish between the progress of religion and the progress of culture in general because the Messiah implies nothing less than a concept of world history. Nevertheless, we shall limit our brief survey to the progress of religion alone.

Wherever religion is closely linked to a personality, it faces a major problem: it is in danger of being mythologized. For myth means basically a personification of the non-personal. The fact that Judaism does not expect the hoped-for and ultimate divine act—unification of God's children in harmony and faithfulness—to be accomplished by a person shows how different it is from myth. The temptation to envisage such a person would have been great enough because Israel's patriotic heart and mind had long been filled with a yearning for a scion of David's. Yet the logic of Judaism's basic religious principle prevailed. Thus, the image of King David as the Messiah was expunged, to be replaced by "Yahweh's servant" who, with Israel—or the "remnant of Israel"—as intermediary, can be none but the people of the future or future mankind. And while the Messiah had originally denoted a dynastic person, the inner development of this thought resulted in the abolition of any personality cult. That is, even with regard to monotheism's ultimate objective, all hero-cult as such and particularly any cult of a divine person was given up.

By now, all educated men believe that this is the real meaning of Judaism's Messianic idea, though they do not yet acknowledge the implications of this sublime thought for their own Messianic concept. Eventually, they will have to rise to this insight. For the moral mankind of an historical future, and it alone, is the "Anointed of the Lord," the Messiah. Taking into consideration the true meaning of the term "Messiah," we must therefore state that its translation as "Christ" is no longer tenable. For the Messiah was never envisioned as effecting the individual's redemption from sin nor was his coming expected to achieve this individuated religious goal. According to the prophets' teachings, man himself, assisted by religion, must accomplish his salvation. But the world's salvation, mankind's advancement, its purification from sins committed throughout history, and the establishment of universal peace under God and in faithfulness and justice—all of these constitute tasks to which any individual effort must forever remain unequal.

These tasks, however, signify an ultimate concern with the practicability of morality. For ethics must not remain a lovely abstraction; it must be concretized into valid truth. At this point, ethics joins forces with religion because ethics too has ultimately no other recourse but to hypothesize the idea of God: not for the personal redemption of the moral individual but as a guarantee for the eventual realization of morality in this world.

The Messianic Idea

Even the most severe modern moralists do not deny the validity of one particular human emotion and its justification: hope. Yet such a positive evaluation of hope is by no means common to all ages or all nations. In fact, the appraisal of this human affect might well be regarded as the criterion for determining not just the psychological differences between men, but the difference between a polytheistic and a monotheistic faith.

To the earliest Greeks, hope meant no more than idle speculation. And it is only after the Persian wars that this emotion is looked on as more than the opposite of fear, or as one of Pandora's evils. From then on, the term appears here and there in the sense of religious faith. But even during the Golden Age of Greece, the word simply connotes a sense of personal relief, affecting the imagination of the poor or unhappy individual. Nowhere in paganism does the concept of hope suggest a general enhancement of all human existence. This widening-out into the non-personal, ethical realm, this spiritualization of a basically materialistic-personalistic emotion is the effect and indeed one of the surest marks of the idea of God's unity or—what amounts to the same thing—of His pure spirituality. In Old Testament usage, hope and faith are identical. The last word of the dying patriarch: "In Thy own time do I place my hope," [1] makes salvation the substance of hope, and hope the guarantee of salvation. As "hope and future," hope is therefore the highest reward the prophet can promise; and it is the mood underlying the psalmist's religious faith: "I hope for the Lord; my soul hopes, more than watchmen hope for the morning." [2]

How did the Israelites accomplish this spiritualization, this conceptual purification that the idealistic Greeks never achieved despite all their art and their patriotism? True, hope is not consonant with the mood of Greek drama. Its tragedy is predicated on fear and compassion, its comedy on the very opposite of hope, namely irony. Yet no matter how much we may appreciate the Greeks' great aesthetic achievements, we find only a negative explanation for their lack of hope.

To put it positively, hope is the product as well as the expression of faith in divine providence. And divine providence means neither a concern, first and foremost, with the individual nor exclusively with one's own people, but rather with all mankind as the children of God. Hope for one's own well-being is conducive to vanity. Hope for the well-being and continued existence of one's own people, though possibly conducive to the development of courage and a sacrificial spirit, easily engenders pride as well. And when one's own country experiences a prolonged period of distress, all hope seems to be vain, adding merely to one's sense of frustration and dejection.

But man's hope is transformed into faith when he no longer thinks of himself alone, that is, of his salvation here and now, or of his eternal salvation (the latter, if I may say so, with calculating sanctimoniousness). Hope is transformed into faith when man associates the future with the emergence of a community whose

1. Probably a reference to and adaptation of Genesis 49:18.
2. This is a rendition of Cohen's free translation of Psalms 130:5, 6.

concerns will reach beyond its everyday concrete reality. Such a community will not be composed merely of man's immediate circle of friends or family nor will it include only those who share his own cherished beliefs; indeed, it will even cut across the borders of his own country because it will represent the community of mankind. As faith in mankind, Israel's faith is hope. And it is this epitome of Israel's prophetism, this hope in mankind's future, that comprises the substance of the Messianic idea. . . .

All ideas, even the most profound which eventually conquer the world, originate within the narrow confines of nationality and are conditioned by the spirit of the times, and even by the contingencies of personality. At its inception, the universal Messianic idea has, as it were, clearly visible national seams as well as many associations quite incongruent with its basic tendency, its concept of divine providence. But while historical evaluations must never cover up weakness in an idea or the false turns it occasionally takes throughout its various developmental stages, they must also never lose sight of the ultimate goal it tries to approximate. For without such a goal, it loses its value as an idea, that is to say, as a model and guiding principle for world history. . . .

The term Messiah, which originally had a political connotation, underwent several transformations and transmutations of meaning. "Messiah" means "the Anointed." At first, this was the title of the priest, whose functions included the anointing of the king. Later, this appellation shifted to the king himself as the object of the priest's ministrations. Subsequent to the people's sad realization that there could also be bad kings, however, this traditional mark of distinction was no longer restricted to a primarily political or national usage; given a new meaning, it was transferred to the people as a whole, a nation of priests.

Because this transfer was accomplished by the prophet, he too is called the Messiah. Yet a sense of patriotic piety survives along with the nation's memory of its golden age. In poetic reminiscences, the good kings, Hezekiah and, above all, David—as a poet, David is also regarded as a prophet—were still associated with the idea of a Messiah long after it ceased to be a political concept. But presently the Messiah, son of David and official functionary, having changed from priest to king and from prophet to people, turns into the bearer of an historical idea.

We call this idea historical in the sense that it becomes the guiding principle of history, and by no means merely of national history. For though the political assumption that the Messiah would be Israel's redeemer still affects the patriotic emotions of the people, the prophet gradually comes to see the Jewish state, the kingdom of David, and the city of Jerusalem as God's kingdom on earth. Thus, the Messiah, designated to establish this kingdom of God, is now no longer regarded as a political emissary but rather as the guarantor of a faith which believes that divine postulates are realizable on earth. And this gives to the Messianic idea its eminent historical significance.

Moreover, the Messiah, once his image has changed, is no longer subject to the ambiguities of hero worship. True, at first he still remains a person; but this personal concept gradually vanishes, transmuted into the symbol of an era. To put it bluntly, the Messiah becomes a calendar concept, and this will later be referred to as "the days of the Messiah." The anointed is thus transfigured into the idea of an historical era of mankind.

Certain political factors contribute to this disposition to give up a political-national principle in favor of a humanitarian and genuinely religious concept. Indeed, the coming of the Messiah is predicated not on the flourishing of the state but on its destruction. And this destruction, the prophet proclaims, will be brought about as the punishment for and divine judgment of a way of life indulged in by the chosen people and its political leaders that makes a mockery of his teachings. These prophetic exhortations would seem seditious; yet they are indispensable as manifestations of the new Messianic concept. The people must be made to understand that they will be ready to receive the comfort and consolation commonly regarded as proper Messianic functions only after they have lost their statehood. That is, they will have to live through a period of national mourning and repentance before the Messiah will restore them as a nation. And they will be restored for a purpose: the renewed glorification of the divine name.

The people's restoration, then, must be seen not merely as a political or national goal but as an apostolic task. And it also becomes quite clear that a political uprising, though originally fervently hoped for and self-confidently advocated, is after all nothing but a secondary means to attain the ultimate goal: the acknowledgment of God's unity by all men. . . .

In contradistinction to natural history, human history is an account of the development of moral beings. Man becomes moral when his actions are no longer self-serving but goal-oriented. A nutshell containing a moral idea comprises the entire kingdom of heaven. The throne of David represents no moral goal but serves at best as a means to attain such a goal. And a scion of this royal house can at best turn into a legendary figure of historical significance. But the Messianic idea offers man the consolation, confidence, and guarantee that not merely the chosen people but all nations will, at some future time, exist in harmony, as nature does today.

Now, this would appear to be a contradiction in terms if it were not meant simply to convey a mental image. And what this image means to express is an attempt to adapt the concept of time to that of morality: we see that the present is characterized by continual change; and for all we know, this change may be necessary. But must it always remain like that? Should there not be some time-to-come, a future which deserves to remain unchanged? Can we not imagine a time of such abiding and enduring moral ethos that we might or should ascribe eternity to it? This is what is meant by the expression "some time, at the end of days"; and this is what is meant by the Messianic idea.

It is said that knowledge of God will result in virtue, and fulfillment of the divine commandments in well-being and peace. Yet neither the one nor the other can in itself guarantee a Messianic future. The actualization of that time-to-come constitutes a specific task, inferred from the insight that there is no need for men to be forever engaged in a struggle for existence. The fact that things are today as they were yesterday does not necessarily mean that they have to be like that tomorrow. Nor need the future be envisaged as a repetition of the past or as shrouded in mythological twilight.

Rather, the future is a postulate of religious faith and indeed its most wondrous flower. . . . .

We therefore believe that the Messianic idea is the culmination as well as the touchstone of religion and that religious conviction means Messianic religiosity.

CHAPTER 4

Reason and Moral Awareness

Editor's Note

Human morality has a spiritual dimension. To develop a sense of moral awareness, man must draw upon his reason. But his reason is not self-attained, a faculty acquired by his own effort. Reason is an endowment of God, bestowed by the Creator on His creature as a truly humanizing mark of distinction.

To say that God endowed man with reason is to say that He inspirited him by revealing to him His own holy spirit, His spirit of holiness. Cohen feels that the term "holy spirit" is almost redundant because all spirit is "holy", an ideality distinct though by no means separate from all reality. God's holiness signifies His absolute spirituality, His unique immateriality. And man's (postulated) holiness represents an "ought," an ethical task demanding his never-to-be-abandoned striving for moral perfection.

Reason, as revealed divine—that is, holy—spirit establishes a correlation between God the Creator and man the creature: God relates Himself to man through the dual act of creation and revelation by which He imparts His spirit of holiness to man. And man relates himself to God by trying to become "holy." This means that the morally aware individual makes full use of his reason by a constant renewal or re-creation of his God-given spirit: he sanctifies himself, as it were, through a way of life that attempts to approximate God's holiness. Reason then becomes the mediator between God and man; as he sanctifies himself, man sanctifies God and thus "accomplishes" God's holiness.

Reason, spirit, and holiness inhere conjointly in both God and man. Yet though God and man are of necessity conceptually correlated, they must of equal necessity remain conceptually distinct. Normative Judaism totally rejects any notion of a mystical union between God and man. In fact, it even hesitates to make any definitive statement about man's immortality, that is, about the fate of his spirit (alias soul) after the death of his body.

But inasmuch as nothing transitory can issue from God, immortality, understood in an entirely immaterial sense, might be considered a logical consequence of the Biblical concept that God created man's spirit. "The soul's return to God represents the consummation of the relationship of God and man," says Cohen. In the metaphorical language of the Psalms this is called "nearness of God," which is felt to be not only man's "greatest good" or "most precious possession" but the culmination of all his hopes and efforts.

Though "nearness of God" is a poetic term describing a manifestly religious concept, "trust in God," in Cohen's interpretation, is not an exclusively religious concept but also an ethical postulate. For when religion refers to trust in God and ethics (the very core of all philosophy, for Cohen) to the apperception of an idea, they differ only methodologically. Substantively, they mean the same thing because religion and ethics alike must "trust in God as the guarantor of the establishment of morality on earth." In Cohen's view, the God-idea is as fundamental to ethics as it is to religion because it comprises both well-spring and ultimate goal of all morality.

Reason, the Hallmark of
Divine Creation

God endowed man with reason, which he could not have attained by himself, for reason is the hallmark of divine creation. Through reason man becomes the image of God.

And God can have bestowed upon man only the same reason, no matter how different in degree, that constitutes His own divine essence. Thus reason establishes a relation between God and man which, though far from indicating their identity, is consistent with the original meaning of pantheism.

Creation and revelation, both implying reason, represent one and the same function of God. As the Creator of his reason, God is the Creator of man. Hence, all creation is also revelation for it is the awakening and unfolding of divine reason in man.

The Holy Spirit

The term "holy spirit," as used in the title of this essay, is an inaccurate rendition of the Hebrew words *ruah hakodesh;* the error is due to a misconception with regard to the true meaning of these words. The correct translation is "the spirit of holiness." What is the difference between these two formulations? To answer this question, we must first examine the concepts "spirit" and "holiness" separately, and then look at both of them together in the word-combination "spirit of holiness."

1. Spirit and Soul. God and Man. Morality and Holiness. The Hebrew terms for "spirit" and "holy" have a long and almost parallel history; both are indicative of the innermost development of Biblical religion.

"Spirit" is originally the same as "wind" or "breath of life." But both these designations come to mean and continue to mean the spirit of God. For it is God who rules the winds and makes the earth come into and pass out of existence. "Spirit" also becomes "the God of the spirits of all flesh" (Numbers, 16:22;27:16), and thus the soul of the body; and the soul was understood to have been created by God in the body and for the body.

As the concept "soul" assumes an ever greater significance in religious thinking, its inner relationship to morality and to all that is spiritual becomes more immediate. Hence, "spirit" is now vari-

ously linked to all the spiritual and moral characteristics and activities of the soul. These attributes of the soul, however, reach their
ultimate perfection in a concept that comes to be the quintessence
of the attributes of God; and this ideal concept—of the human
soul as well as of God—is designated as "holiness."

Thus, the very origin of the concepts "spirit" and "holiness"
already implies that they inhere conjointly in both man and God.

God is the Creator, the Molder of the spirit of man. Hence,
spirit relates God to man, and man to God.

God is the holy God, and He considers man worthy of receiving
His commandment: "Ye shall be holy; for I the Lord your God am
holy" (Leviticus 19:2). Therefore holiness also relates God to
man, and man to God.

2. Rarity of the Term. Obviously, the combination of the terms
"spirit" and "holiness" represents an intensification of this relation. It might therefore seem strange that this combination, this
appellation "the spirit of holiness" occurs in our Bible only three
times: twice in a passage in Isaiah (63:10,11),[1] and once in
Psalms (51:13).[2] Could it be that the formulation was considered
redundant? Or might this reticence in using the term reveal a providential cautiousness?

The Isaiah passage will show us that the term "spirit of holiness"
adds no fundamentally new element to the concept "spirit of God."
For insofar as the latter already implies holiness, it is conceptually
identical with the former. And this identity extends also to the
correlation of God and man. God is spirit and God is holy. Hence,
He must impart to man both spirit and holiness and through them
relate Himself to man. Thus God's spirit of holiness is equally
man's spirit of holiness. The consequence of this identity is simple
and clear; yet the great import of the original concept gives rise to
an abundance of new conclusions.

The reference to the spirit of holiness in verse 13 of Psalm 51

1. "But they rebelled, and grieved His holy spirit . . . Where is He that
put His holy spirit in the midst of them?"
2. "Cast me not away from Thy presence; And take not Thy holy spirit
from me."

establishes a more intimate relationship between God and man. What is its nature?

Actually, this passage too adds no new element to either the concept of God or that of man. Yet it makes explicit what was previously merely implicit in the development of the terms "spirit" and "holiness"; and the fact that it is the only passage of its kind does not at all diminish its importance.

What is new, however, in this wonderful passage is the poignancy with which it juxtaposes God's spirit of holiness and man's sinfulness. And it is characteristic of the Psalms—of their style as well as their notion of sin and redemption—that they, and they alone, create this term (though seemingly for this one occasion only) as they explore the question of man's existence and his relationship to God. Let us follow the above-mentioned development in some detail.

3. *Spirit.* The term "spirit" primarily implies a contrast to all matter and therefore also to all physical being. But this contrast is not felt to represent an irreconcilable conflict. Spirit and matter are rather seen as interconnected in every living thing and therefore particularly in man. And this interconnection of the spiritual and physical in man establishes the link between God and man. For spirit means God, not only soul.

The concept of spirit must necessarily be associated with the concept of God. For God represents first and foremost a contrast to all forces of nature. He is neither in the wind nor in the fire (I Kings 19:11,12). And by the same token, the divine spirit represents a contrast to all human might, especially military might (Zechariah 4:6). And from this specific divine spirituality follow the concepts of God's omniscience and omnipresence: "Whither shall I go from Thy spirit? Or whither shall I flee from Thy presence?" (Psalms 139:7).

With the increasing spiritualization of the concept of God goes an increasing inwardness of the relation between God and man. We saw this development already anticipated in the notion that every living organism is inspirited: "He is the God of the spirits of all flesh" (Numbers 16:22;27:16). But already in these two passages "spirit" means not merely the spirit of life; it implies an entire spiritual dimension—hence, and ever more definitely, God's complete dominance over man.

4. Creation. This providential relationship not only between God and man but between God and all nature is intrinsic to the concept of creation. God and man are linked correlatively: God must create man. And if this is true with regard to man as such, it is particularly true with regard to his spirit or specifically his soul: "In whose hand is the soul of every living thing" (Job 12:10).

For Job, however, not only physical existence nor even reason alone are derived from the spirit of God. He feels—and so secure is he in his belief that he clothes it in the form of a rhetorical question—that man's inheritance from God constitutes his spiritual autonomy: "For what [else] would be the portion of God from above, and the heritage of the Almighty from on high?" (Job 31:2). Here, the two words designating an inherited portion (*helek venaḥalah*) are used to express the feeling that the human mind has a full and legitimate share in God. It is as if Job meant to say: "My spirit is part of the deity's creation from above, and it is the heritage the Almighty has apportioned to me from on high." The abstract appellations for God, "deity" and "the Almighty," and the concrete designations which refer to the origin of the human spirit, "from above" and "from on high" may, when taken together, be seen as indicative of a tendency to trace the origin of the whole man back to God, or to ground man's total being in the mystery that is God. Let us pursue this thought further.

God the Creator becomes the molder of man's heart and spirit. "He that fashioneth the hearts of them all" (Psalms 33:15), and He "who stretched forth the heavens, and laid the foundation of the earth, and formed the spirit of man within him" (Zechariah 12:1). As the calling-into-being of heaven and earth is a special act of creation, so is the forming of man's spirit within him.

5. God's Responsibility for Man. Through His act of creation, God becomes responsible for man. And since the concept of God is associated with intellect and morality, "spirit" now appears in the context of man's intellectual or moral activities. Job rightfully places particular emphasis on God's creation of the life-giving spirit in man: "The spirit of God hath made me, and the breath of the Almighty giveth me life" (Job 33:4). He realizes, however, that not merely the life-giving quality of the spirit is grounded in God but its intellectual quality as well: "But it is a spirit in man, and the breath of the Almighty, that giveth them understanding" (Job 32:8).

Our myths already trace the intellectual nature of man's spirit back to God. From Him comes the art of Bezalel; and Joseph and Joshua, all the Judges, Samson the hero as well as Saul and the prophets—they were all given their wisdom and their artistry by God.

6. *The Spirit of God in the Messiah.* The spirit of God also gives authenticity to the Messiah. And while this spirit is described elsewhere as "Thy good spirit" (Nehemiah 9:20; Psalms 143:10), this is what is said about it in connection with the Messiah: "And the spirit of the Lord shall rest upon him, the spirit of wisdom and understanding, the spirit of counsel and might, the spirit of knowledge and the fear of the Lord" (Isaiah 11:2). More moral faculties of the spirit cannot be comprised even in the Messiah.

7. *The Spirit of God with Reference to the People.* Spirit, however, relates to God not only man as an individual but also the people of Israel, and particularly the prophets. Yet in matters of the spirit there are to be no distinctions among the people. "Would that all the Lord's people were prophets, that the Lord would put His spirit upon them!" (Numbers 11:29). This original universalism of the spirit, as conceived by Israel, leads to Messianism and finds its ultimate expression in it. In Isaiah, the entire earth is to be filled with an understanding of the Lord. And in Jeremiah, all differences in the degree of human understanding are to be obliterated: "For they shall all know Me, from the least of them unto the greatest of them" (Jeremiah 31:34). The final consequence of this thought is found in Joel: "I will pour out My spirit upon

all flesh . . . and also upon the servants and upon the hand-
maids" (Joel 3:1,2).

Thus, Ezekiel's prophecy for the house of Israel becomes a truth
in the Messianic sense: "A new heart also will I give you, and a
new spirit will I put within you . . . And I will put My spirit
within you" (Ezekiel 36:26,27); and "For I have poured out My
spirit upon the house of Israel, saith the Lord God" (Ezekiel
39:29).

8. Immortality. Koheleth's skepticism led him to express the
thought: "Who knoweth the spirit of man whether it goeth up-
ward, and the spirit of the beast whether it goeth downward to the
earth?" (Ecclesiastes 3:21). But confronted with the idea of Messianism, no skepticism can persist; and thus we shall see how this
mood is also overcome in Koheleth.

Contemplating the nature of that bond which the spirit establishes between God and man, we might find it incomprehensible
that immortality has not become an explicit tenet of monotheism.
"Into Thy hand I commit my spirit" (Psalms 31:6). True, an old
prayer adds: ". . . and my body along with my spirit." Still, this
naive confession of concern for his physical well-being by the poet
does not contradict the desire to commit one's spirit, above all,
to God's eternal care. Nevertheless, this old prayer shows why the
notion of the human spirit's immortality had to be offensive to a
truly absolute monotheism.

For can it be true, in any sense whatever, that man should be
everlasting when it is God alone who is called the Eternal? And
does the myth of immortality not recapitulate the notion—originally set forth in the story of the Garden of Eden—of an eternal
life for man?

Our Bible wisely modifies this notion by making it congruent
with the precept of the spirit's origin in God. Koheleth's solution
of this problem seems the most sublime: "And the dust returneth
to the earth as it was, and the spirit returneth unto God who gave
it" (Ecclesiastes 12:7). Has the notion of immortality ever been
interpreted in a more positive sense, or was it ever given a meaning
of greater poignancy or simpler purity than that communicated by
this devout utterance?

The human spirit is by no means transfigured into a divine spirit after death, however; it remains the spirit of man. Nor does it become one with God; rather it becomes once more what it always has been: God's creation. God constitutes its home. He has (as pointed out before) "formed the spirit of man within him" (Zechariah 12:1); but the Creator of man's spirit had put it into man's body. Now that the body returns to the earth to which as dust it belongs, the spirit returns to God, from whom it has come.

Is there any doctrine of immortality that can say anything more simple yet definitive about man's fate after death? He has come from God and returns to God. From the very beginning, man is bound up with God; and this bond continues to exist, unaffected by death which befalls the body only. God's creation of man's spirit, then, must be understood as a principle whose consequence is immortality.

Through this creation, the correlation of God and man—a prerequisite inherent in the concept "spirit"—is established and maintained. And while "spirit" here means spirit of man, it is God who has bestowed it upon him and who is responsible for it and its preservation. But since nothing transitory can issue from God, the human spirit must return to Him once the individual form of man's earthly existence is dissolved.

More than that we are not told, for monotheism refrains from making any definite statement or from engaging in any speculation about life after death. The psalmist is content to voice his confidence: "Every soul praises God" (Psalms 150:6).[3] And the fact that this is the concluding statement of the Psalms is characteristic of their approach to the problem. The kind of praise meant here can be rendered only by the soul, only by the spirit: "Shall the dust praise Thee? shall it declare Thy truth?" (Psalms 30:10). And it was the psalmist too who unearthed this treasure-trove of the soul: "Whom have I in heaven but Thee? And beside Thee I desire none upon earth; . . . the nearness of God is my good" (Psalms 73:25;28). And in this "nearness of God" an ancient thinker already saw the best surrogate for immortality.

True, once returned to God, the soul can no longer engage in

3. This is Cohen's rendition; the J.P.S. translation reads: "Let everything that hath breath praise the Lord."

any other form of moral activity. But if only his soul can praise God and enjoy His nearness, if only it can persevere in its love of and reverence for Him, the psalmist's religious yearning is so completely satisfied that he sees man's return to God as the fulfillment of his most fervent desire, the realization of his ultimate hope, and the goal of all human existence. Thus, the cycle of the spirit's origin in and return to God is the best guarantee of its immortality. Any other positive statement about immortality would constitute a reversion from religion to mythology. But having made this qualification, one might say that the soul's return to God represents the consummation of the relationship of God and man without leading to an obliteration of their respective distinctiveness.

9. Holiness as Separateness. As we proceed to a discussion of the concept "holiness," we must remember the earliest primitive meaning attached to this notion in the sacrificial service. In ancient mythology, any place, person, animal, building or utensil could be set apart from the community or common usage and regarded as holy; and this feeling that separateness signified holiness was further intensified in connection with the sacrificial service performed in the sanctuary by the priest.

Yet ever since Abraham resisted the cult of the Sabaens,[4] monotheism developed another conception of holiness, in a straight line of historical continuity. Out of the myths that dominated all thought and ceremony, all speech and conviction, there emerged this parallelism: "Ye shall be holy; for I the Lord your God am holy" (Leviticus 19:2). With this correlation, the mythic meaning of holiness was all at once converted into a new meaning of morality.

10. Holiness as Task. A mythic version of this Biblical passage would read: "Ye shall become holy, for I will make you holy." But in the Bible, God demands man's holiness. He makes holiness man's task. And the charging with this task as well as its execu-

---

4. A Semitic people frequently referred to in the Bible, who inhabited the southwest of the Arabian peninsula, worshiping the stars, sun and moon.

tion are contingent solely upon the correlation of God and man, a correlation defined nowhere as distinctly and unequivocally as here. "Ye shall be holy, for I am holy." That is, correlation is prerequisite to the task; otherwise, the reason given for the task would make no sense. And should one, moreover, not assume that by definition only God can be holy, while man by definition cannot attain holiness?

Man can indeed not be at all sure that he will attain holiness; yet his task as such remains. While God's holiness is an accomplished fact, man's holiness lies in the realm of the "ought." God's demand for man's sanctification is justified by and predicated upon their correlation which necessitates as well as makes possible the linkage of God and man in holiness.

11. Spiritualization of Man's Service and Knowledge of God. The increasingly profound meaning given to the notion of holiness—beginning with the setting-apart of objects or a separating-out of material things as such and proceeding first to a renunciation of all that is worldly (insofar as it is selfish) and then to moral purification—is the natural result of the spiritualization of the concepts of God and man. And this development corresponds, in turn, to a process in which service and knowledge of God come to represent the highest ideals of man.

12. Sabbath Legislation. The Sabbath symbolizes the high standard of social ethics prevailing in the life of the Israelites. "Happy is the man . . . that keepeth the Sabbath from profaning it, and keepeth his hand from doing any evil" (Isaiah 56:2). And connected with this idea of the Sabbath are all the socio-agrarian Sabbath laws whose culmination is the institution of the jubilee year.

13. Messianism. But the final stage in the development of Jewish social ethics and of the concept of God's and man's correlation is represented by Messianism. God will send the Messiah, who is the end product of all historical existence and represents the hope and trust of all national existence. From this idea evolves the notion that the people of Israel, the "remnant of Israel," is comprised of the righteous, that is to say, of the poor. Subsequently, this remnant itself is called "the servant of the Lord" and thus becomes the Messiah. The designation "remnant of Israel" undergoes still another conceptual change, however, and assumes a still broader meaning. It now stands for the brotherhood of man embracing all nations that "follow the Lord." Thus, there emerges—as a corollary of the concept of the Messiah—a concept of man who, freed from all distinctions of origin, embodies that unity of the one mankind consistent with the unity of the One God.

Having followed the notions so far discussed through their various phases of development, we must now examine the corresponding development of the concept "holiness" as it refers to God and to man.

14. The Holy God. Universalism. Monotheism and the Being of God. God is holy; that is to say: God is the Holy One. Among the many spiritual and moral attributes constituting the concept of God none is as central as that of holiness. Holiness is the quintessence of all God's attributes. He is "the Holy One of Israel," and as such He shall be called "the God of the whole earth" (Isaiah 54:5).

The concept of holiness, divorced now from all mythic connotations, even serves to counteract anthropomorphism. Thus the "holy God" becomes "the name of holiness" (Ezekiel 39:7). "And all flesh will praise the name of My holiness" (Psalms 145:21).[5]

Holiness of and through the divine name, then, implies universalism as well as monotheism. "There is none holy as the Lord; for there is none beside Thee" (I Samuel 2:2).

Holiness becomes identical with the being of God as such and is equated with His nature: "To whom then will ye liken Me, that I should be equal? Saith the Holy One" (Isaiah 40:25). Hence, the theophany in Isaiah consists in the calling out, three times over, of the word "holy" (Isaiah 6:3).

"Yet Thou art holy, O Thou that are enthroned upon the praises

5. These are Cohen's renditions of the text which reads in the J.P.S. translation: "My holy name" and: "And let all flesh bless His holy name forever and ever," respectively.

of Israel" (Psalms 22:4). This passage (which Graetz,[6] discerning as ever, finds strange) may well be explained by the changed and broadened meaning of the concept holiness. For now God is no longer conceived of as dwelling in Zion, His holy mountain (Joel 4:17), or in His holy habitation, in heaven (Deuteronomy 26:15), or in His holy Temple (Psalms 138:2) or His holy place (Psalms 24:3). Over against all these localities—no matter how spiritual in conception—there is now set Israel's acknowledgement of God; with this, the basic principle of God's and man's correlation is established. "The praises of Israel" have replaced the notion of Zion and all that goes with it.

Eventually and logically the concept of Israel's and God's correlation is extended and is applied now to all other nations as well: "And the nations shall know that I am the Lord, the Holy One in Israel" (Ezekiel 39:7). Israel's holy God—the inference here is that God must be acknowledged by all the peoples of the earth. Ultimately, holiness is associated with Messianism too: "And the Holy One of Israel is thy Redeemer, the God of the whole earth shall He be called" (Isaiah 54:5).

And finally, holiness (in addition to spirit) is associated with the concept of the Creator who is now designated as "the Holy One": "The Holy One of Israel and his Maker" (Isaiah 45:11). The notion that both Israel and mankind originate in God's holiness gives added significance to the concept of correlation.

15. Transference of the Concept "Holiness" to Man. And now we must consider the transference of the concept "holiness" to man, within the qualifications of the commandment.

In connection with the concept of God, the idea evolves: "God the Holy One is sanctified through righteousness" (Isaiah 5:16). That means that the correlation between God's holiness and man is established through the latter's righteousness, that highest expression of morality. Subsequently, God's sanctification becomes man's task, as evidenced by the commandment: "And ye shall sanctify Me." [7]

This injunction is analogous to the passage: "I will be hallowed

6. Heinrich Graetz, 1817–1891, author of *History of the Jews.*
7. A reference to and adoption of Numbers 27:14, "To sanctify Me."

among the children of Israel" (Leviticus 22:32). God's sanctification is accomplished by man. And man, in turn, fulfills his striving
for holiness by acknowledging the ideal of holiness, God, whom he
tries to emulate and by whose emulation he himself is sanctified.
"Sanctify yourselves therefore, and be ye holy" (Leviticus 11:44).
Holiness as sanctification thus permeates the correlation of God
and man, fulfilling a requisite inherent in the concept of God and
enhancing the concept of man by charging him with the task, and
imbuing him with the ability, to strive for holiness.

As spirit relates God to man and man to God, so does holiness.
Yet the distinction between God and man remains inviolate. God
does not become man, and man does not become God. The fact that
God and man remain distinct does, however, not imply that they
remain unbridgeably apart: the idea of holiness establishes and
guarantees their relationship. Indeed, the principle of holiness, as
applied to God, would seem to lack purpose if it were not also
applied to man and put into practice by him.

16. Analogy between Spirit and Holiness. Self-Sanctification.
The sentence: "I am the Lord who sanctify you" (Leviticus 20:
8;21:8) implies an analogy between spirit and holiness. As God
endows man with spirit, so does He imbue him with holiness. This
is no invalidation of the thought expressed in the commandment:
"Sanctify yourselves therefore, and be ye holy" (Leviticus 11:44).
For even self-sanctification means intrinsically the bestowal of
holiness by God. This must, however, not be understood in the
sense that God imparts some of His own holiness to man; it suggests rather that God demands self-sanctification of man. The interpretation in *Siphra* [8] is therefore based on a correct exegesis.

Hence the analogy to the statement: "I sanctify you" is the commandment: "The Lord of hosts, Him shall ye sanctify" (Isaiah
8:13). This commandment is wholly consonant with the concept
of correlation. God is to be sanctified; that means His name must
be proclaimed. This is already a postulate of the Torah and of
early Jewish tradition which sees no sin in Moses other than his
failure to comply with this command as he strikes the rock; and
in Messianism God's sanctification through man is fully achieved.

8. *Siphra* (Book), A Halakhic Midrash (interpretation) on Leviticus.

17. The Holy Spirit. The analogy between spirit and holiness brings us at last to the concept "the holy spirit."

In an oratory of magnificent beauty, the author of the Isaiah text suddenly mentions the holy spirit for the first time in the old canon, and in two consecutive verses. The first reference seems rather random. After recounting that "in His love and in His pity He redeemed them; and He bore them, and carried them all the days of old," the author goes on to say: "But they rebelled, and grieved His holy spirit" (Isaiah 63:9,10). There is no apparent reason for the choice of this new term here. To be grieved, God needs no holy spirit. But immediately afterwards, as the people continues to recall the days of old, the text reads: "Where is He that put His holy spirit in the midst of them?" (Isaiah 63:11).

Now, the inner connection between the designation "holy spirit" and the concept "spirit" as such becomes evident. For it is God who puts the spirit into man or who "formed the spirit of man within him" (Zechariah 12:1). Here, then, "spirit" is understood in the correct sense—as having been put into us, into man, by God. And it is in this sense that the Isaiah text speaks of the holy spirit as having been put in the midst of the people.

The holy spirit then is not different from spirit as such. And the sudden appearance of this term in a passage that does not convey any new religious truth remains a literary mystery.

18. The Holy Spirit and Sin. Now we come to the single other mention of the holy spirit, in Psalm 51. This is a true penitential psalm, full of contrition though also of hope for forgiveness. The mood of repentance gripping the author of this penitential prayer may account for its opening line: ". . . after he had gone in to Bath-sheba." This possibility is not ruled out by verse 6, which says: "Against Thee, Thee only have I sinned." For this confession merely expresses the psalmist's profound awareness that all sins committed against another human being fade into insignificance compared to a sin committed against God.

At first, the poet voices his uneasiness concerning his own existence: "Behold, I was brought forth in iniquity, and in sin did my mother conceive me" (verse 7). This verse should not be understood as a reference to original sin (in fact, even Christian authors have not had the poor taste to imply any such thing). The poet merely intends to uncover, without false pity, man's moral frailty. The following verse reads: "Behold, Thou desirest truth in the inward parts; make me, therefore, to know wisdom in mine inmost heart." And now there is a cry for God's forgiveness: "Wash me, and I shall be whiter than snow. . . . Do not hide Thy countenance from my sins. . . ." [9] God's pardon can redeem man from his sin.

But the poet does not stop with this prayer for forgiveness; he now turns his attention to his own heart and spirit: "Create me a clean heart, O God; and renew a steadfast spirit within me" (verse 12). This means that neither the state of man's heart nor that of his spirit are determined at birth. Rather, God is asked to recreate man's heart and his spirit because only thus will they become "steadfast." Here, we have a true understanding of the nature of "spirit": it is in need of constant renewal or, in the language of the prayer, God must forever renew it. This constant renewal of man's heart and spirit helps to thwart his inclination to sin and will thus achieve his redemption.

This profound religious insight makes it clear why "spirit" is called "holy spirit." Struggling against his own sinfulness, the poet asks God to stamp out his evil inclination: "Cast me not away from Thy presence; and take not Thy holy spirit from me" (verse 13). To suggest, as has been done, that the term "holy spirit" means "spirit of prophecy" is erroneous. For inasmuch as God has put spirit not only "in the midst of" the people but also in the individual, every human being, not the prophet alone, must be considered inspirited.

By the same token every man is holy, for holiness is a task incumbent upon every individual. God wishes to be sanctified by all men. And what is true of "spirit" and of "holiness" taken separately is so much the more true of "the holy spirit," which represents a fusion of those two elements that bring about the correlation of God and man.

The notion of correlation has here reached a stage of profound

9. This is Cohen's rendition. The J.P.S. translation is: ". . . Hide Thy face from my sins . . ."

inwardness. In his prayer for forgiveness, the poet, repenting his sin, evokes God's holy spirit, with which he too has been endowed. It is as if he meant to say: "Once you have given me your holy spirit, you must not take it from me again." And indeed, the holy spirit, given by God to man, remains inalienably his. Sin cannot destory it; sin, however, can be averted by a renewal of man's spirit.

19. Constant Re-Creation by the Holy Spirit. And it may well be that the holy spirit manifests its particular efficacy by its renewal of man's spirit. For man's spirit as such, though put into him by God, might be considered unable to effect its own renewal. But the holy spirit represents that bond between man and God which no sin can sever. God is the Creator of the human spirit. This creation is now understood as a constant re-creation. And re-creation, in turn, keeps alive that sense of holiness in man which, sustained by the holy spirit, culminates in his self-sanctification.

20. No Original Sin. Consequently, the notion of original sin proves untenable and must be overcome; for it contradicts the concept of the holy spirit common to both God and man. This concept represents no new idea at all, as we have shown. It is simply a term indicative of that bond between God and man established through the instrumentality of both holiness and spirit. No sin of man can ever cause God to turn His face from him nor can it rob him of their correlation; for this correlation is intrinsic to the concept of God. And thus the psalmist is justified in pleading that God should not take His holy spirit from him.

21. Not "the" but "Thy" Holy Spirit. It is significant that neither the Psalm nor Isaiah speaks of "the" holy spirit as such. And while it might seem offensive to think of the holy spirit as merely the spirit of man, it is profoundly meaningful to think of it as "Thy holy spirit" or "Thy spirit of holiness" or, perhaps more accurately still, as "the spirit of Thy holiness." For it is God in whom both spirit and holy spirit originate; and it is God who puts both into man.

22. No Personal Intermediary between God and Man. Thus understood, the concept of the holy spirit—besides rendering impossible any notion of original sin—enhances the correlation of God and man. But this correlation is destroyed when the holy spirit is thought of in terms of an autonomous personal intermediary. For the holy spirit can be neither God nor man; nor can it be God and man at once; it is nothing but an attribute, a force, or, so to speak, an instrument of God and man. But if the same holds true, as indeed it does, for spirit and equally so for holiness, how can the holy spirit signify more than a function?

23. Logical Meaning of the Concept "Union." A consideration of the concept of God in connection with that of correlation leads to this new conclusion: God and man must maintain their distinctiveness if they are to be united. Continued distinctiveness [of whatever elements are to be unified] is the premise on which the logical concept of union is based; for unless we predicate union on distinctiveness, we conceive of it in material terms. God is contingent upon His correlation to man, and man is contingent upon his correlation to God. This correlation culminates in the concept of the holy spirit. But here too God must remain God, and man man—if, that is, we think of the holy spirit as common to both; if we think of it as signifying man's sanctification through the spirit of God and God's sanctification through the spirit of man: if, in short, the correlation of God and man is to be conceived as their union in the holy spirit.

24. Union, not Mediation. It is easy to see why this conception of the holy spirit underwent a damaging transformation once correlation was no longer thought of in the uncompromising terms of absolute monotheism. First of all, there existed only those few isolated references to the holy spirit. But secondly, the idea of a union of God and man—and this is what correlation really means—came to be replaced by the vague, utterly imprecise concept of mediation.

Among all the objections raised against Judaism by Christianity in particular but also by pantheism and mysticism, none was probably as detrimental to a fair assessment of Judaism's cultural value as the assertion that it precludes any close relation of God and man. We have therefore attempted to show that the real relation of God and man, namely their true union, as a logical concept, is guaranteed by that holy spirit which inheres in both. No other relation can be conceived of as union.

25. Ambiguities of Spinoza's System. This exposition, then, should serve as a complete refutation of pantheism. Spinoza's toying with the term "holy spirit" is well known. He sometimes equates it—as the spirit of Christ—with divine wisdom. But every so often and in keeping with a basic pantheistic principle, he also equates the holy spirit with human spirit as such, insofar as human spirit partakes of divine wisdom. He fails, however, to take into consideration the fact that the human spirit partakes of God's wisdom only to a certain extent. Moreover, it is doubtful whether even the most adequate kind of human cognitive knowledge could ever be truly identical with divine wisdom. But this question turns on the distinction that must be made between cognitive knowledge and ethics, and Spinoza does not acknowledge the existence of such a distinction.

26. Limitation of the Concept of the Holy Spirit to the Moral Dimension. The Biblical conception of a union of God and man through the instrumentality of the holy spirit is superior to all pantheistic thinking. For monotheism limits the domain of the holy spirit to the spiritual dimension of holiness or morality. And critical philosophy rests on the recognition that there is a difference between the certitude of scientific knowedge and the certitude of ethics.[10] Pantheism, however, ignores or even denies the existence of this critical and basic difference and finds itself for this reason

10. See "The German and the Jewish Ethos I."

alone in an irreconcilable conflict not only with ethics but also with scientifically reasoned philosophy.

This attitude explains too why philosophizing poets and dilettantes of all persuasions flirt with pantheism. They do not even go to the trouble of acquiring the professional tools indispensable to the pursuit of a philosophy that is based on the methodology of science; they feel confident that they can indulge in their philosophical fancies without such equipment. Spinoza actually pretends that his *Definitions* will suffice to protect him against any suspicion that he is merely engaged in fantasies. Yet there can be no ethics prior to logic or indistinct from it. And it is this distinction between the one and the other which is implicit in the Biblical concept of the holy spirit.

True, this distinction is not explicitly drawn. But the particular object of this spirit and hence also of this mode of cognition is clearly defined: the Holy. For while, for instance, Kant assigns—through his "primacy of practical reason"—greater cognitive value to ethics than to science, the Bible is wholly unconcerned with the latter, delineating only that other dimension, simply yet definitively. Holiness presupposes a particular spirit and morality a particular mode of cognition. And this constitutes the methodological superiority of monotheistic over pantheistic thinking.

27. Judaism's Superiority over Pantheism with Regard to the Concept of the Individual. In Judaism, God and man maintain their respective distinctiveness, as we have shown though they are necessarily correlated. That means, on the one hand, that man's individuality remains intact, and on the other that the concept "spirit of holiness" effects a union between God and man. In contradistinction, both Christianity and pantheism teach that God does not remain God, and man does not remain man. In pantheism, the particular object, hence also the individual, lose their separate identity by being subsumed under the universal: the idea of eternity or of divine substance. Thus, no true union of God and man is possible. Instead, it would seem that the last verdict of this kind of theology and anthropology is a negation or nullification of individual existence. Or can one really speak meaningfully of a union when one of its two constituent members must completely disappear in the brilliant radiance of the eternal?

28. Correspondence of Jewish Monotheism and Ethical Idealism. Conversely, the union of God and man through the holy spirit opens up the widest perspective. Here infinity remains the distinctive mark of the godhead alone. The holy spirit is not also the "spirit of the spirits of all flesh." Substance too constitutes an abiding difference between God and man. Man is a phenomenon, a notion already held by Plato. And if, in Kantian terminology, God is the Thing-in-Itself, He is also the Idea by virtue of the same terminology. And the significance of this Idea lies in its mission to the world of man—which is indeed the world of phenomena but at the same time the world of scientific, hence ethical cognition. Thus, a correspondence between this Kantian theory and the Jewish concept of the holy spirit can be established.[11]

In fact, the concept of the holy spirit constitutes a natural bond between Jewish monotheism and scientific idealism. But where the holy spirit is understood to be a mediating rather than a unifying force, it serves the particular interests of that specifically and exclusively scientific world which cannot tolerate any differentiation between God and man, and thus, in the last analysis, is unable to understand those who profess God's unique Oneness. The Greek spirit—that prototype of a scientific world-orientation—seeks this so-called mediation between God and man. (And the Jew Philo fell victim to this Greek magic, as evidenced by his concept of logos.)

29. The Reason for the Differing Views of Pantheism and Monotheism. But what is the real motivation behind that human desire to bridge the gap between God and man? Why cannot all men share the view of that teacher of the Talmud who said: "He dwells in heaven, and you dwell on earth; therefore let your words be few [read: humble]"? Should our thinking really be completely dominated by that rule of logic which attempts to demonstrate only unity in all existence, or does this very unity not actually presup-

11. See also "Affinities Between the Philosophy of Kant and Judaism."

pose existing differences which are equally demonstrable by a rule of logic? The difference between God and man, moreover, implies an ethical task for monotheism insofar as the realization of morality on earth is the concern of ethics and insofar as ethics can ultimately be validated only by the hypothesis of God. But the concept of this God is necessarily different from the concept of man.

The conflict between monotheism and pantheism is not so much a conflict between religion, on the one hand, and philosophy, on the other, as it is a basic disagreement between two kinds of philosophy: one which does and one which does not require a distinct system of ethics.

True, Jewish philosophers, from the earliest times, have not always been impervious to the lures of pantheism; however, there were invariably other Jewish thinkers who would remonstrate with them for posing a threat to monotheism. It would be interesting to find out whether it was the concept of the holy spirit on which these Jewish opponents of Jewish pantheism based their objections; whether, that is, they were aware that their rejection of pantheism was somehow influenced by the concept of the holy spirit—at once divine and human—which precludes any notion of man's innate sinfulness.

30. The Holy Spirit as the Social Messiah. The holy spirit is a most intriguing concept in the history of religious ideas. We have already touched upon its basic difference from the ideology of Hellenism, a subject we cannot pursue further here. But what do the Talmud and the Midrash have to say about this concept? At first, we encounter everywhere the naive view that God Himself is the holy spirit; or we find that the term is regarded merely as a periphrasis for God, similar to the designation "magnificence" or to that peculiar expression "indwelling" which is a symbolic term for God's being. For as God, according to this symbolic expression, dwells in the world, so does the holy spirit dwell in man, according to another Hebrew word.

But then we find in the Midrash a quotation from Elijah, who is considered the precursor of the Messiah: "I call to witness heaven and earth: whether Israelite or Gentile, man or woman, manservant or maidservant: the holy spirit dwells in all, according to their deeds" (*Tanna de-vei Eliyahu*).[12] That means that the holy spirit is now understood to represent an inspirited mankind which will carry out the Messianic task of removing all national and class distinctions separating men.

Moreover, the holy spirit is held to be related solely to man's actions and not to his cognitive faculties. That is to say, it signifies the spirit of ethics rather than theoretical knowledge and has therefore nothing to do with any so-called metaphysics that would undertake to determine the nature of the deity. The spirit of holiness refers exclusively to the moral concept of man, a view held by the rabbis too.

And consistent with the grandiose development which the concepts "spirit" and "holiness" have undergone, it is now man as such, not merely the Israelite, in whom the holy spirit dwells. "Holy spirit" has come to mean the spirit of God as well as the spirit of mankind. The correlation of God and man is now understood in its Messianic significance. The union of God and man can therefore surely not lead to their fusion. God and man remain distinct; yet their union, accomplished through the holy spirit, becomes much closer.

God's Nearness

In keeping with their poetic style, the Psalms use a metaphorical description of man's relationship to God as an illustration of God's spirituality. A particular term is important here: God's nearness, a concept already emphasized in Deuteronomy: "For what great nation is there, that hath God so nigh unto them, as the Lord our God is whensoever we call upon Him?" (Deuteronomy 4:7) [1] The

12. A Hebrew religious work, probably dating from the tenth century, consisting of moral homilies.
1. See "On the Aesthetic Value of Our Religious Education," p. 157.

term "nearness" is here no longer indicative of that superstition which Jeremiah had to counteract by introducing the concept of a distant God. God's omnipresence has become a firmly established notion. And since God is now thought of as ever-present, man's relationship to Him can safely be defined as nearness, that is, a drawing near. Thus, the idea of proximity—in the sense of approximation, of man's approaching God more closely—assumes great significance.

Genuine monotheism finds it difficult to delineate man's relation to God accurately. The Greek (even the Greek philosopher) does not hesitate to speak in this connection of "assimilation" (*homoiosis*), suggesting an essential similarity or likeness between man and God. One already crosses here the line of demarcation that guards their distinctiveness even if one speaks of similarity rather than likeness. In monotheism, man may not aspire to be like God or even to resemble Him. Nevertheless, any relationship does indeed presuppose homogeneity; to what degree of homogeneity then can we admit without doing violence to the concept of God's uniqueness? This difficult question is solved by the notion of God's nearness (or proximity) to man and its correlate, man's approximation (or drawing-near) to God.

God's nearness provides the final note sounded by Psalm 73, which is important in many respects, including its discussion of the problem of theodicy.

> For I was envious at the arrogant, when I saw the prosperity of the wicked . . . In the trouble of man they are not; neither are they plagued like men. Therefore pride is as a chain about their neck; . . . They have set their mouth against the heavens, . . . And they say: 'How doth God know? And is there any knowledge in the Most High?' Behold, such are the wicked; and they that are always at ease increase riches . . . And when I pondered how I might know this, It was wearisome in mine eyes; . . . Thou wilt guide me with Thy counsel, . . . Whom have I in heaven but Thee? And beside Thee I desire none upon earth. . . . But as for me, the nearness of God is my good (Psalms 73:3–28).

Perplexed about the nature of good and evil, the poet has found the solution to his problem: the nearness of God is man's good.

As long as God is not far from him, man lacks nothing. God's nearness, however, depends on man's attitude too: repentance and atonement, those preconditions for attaining a pure heart, are also the means by which man can draw near to God, that is, acknowledge as well as maintain God's nearness.

Drawing close to God constitutes man's moral activity and provides, at the same time, a safeguard against that mysticism which is a violation of pure monotheism. The nearness of God—but by no means a union with God—is man's highest good. "He is in heaven and you are on earth, therefore let your words be few"— thus warns the Talmud against that effusiveness of prayer which is a concomitant of mysticism. The concept of God's nearness precludes any notion that God and man might be one and the same, or that man might become infinite (which, in turn, would inevitably mean that God can become finite). Hence, the concept of God's nearness serves to preserve that of His spiritual unity.

On the Aesthetic Value of
Our Religious Education

The concept of the Messiah represents not only the fundamental principle of modern ethics (insofar as this is the ethics of the one mankind) but also the source of all religious art. And we may well call the Messianic concept of man the basis of modern aesthetics. It was Kant, however, who first incorporated aesthetics into a philosophical system with the assertion that aesthetics and ethics are closely related. This position was presented to the general educated public by Schiller,[1] whose aesthetics is grounded in two ethical principles: the idea of freedom and that of one mankind. For Kant and Schiller alike, freedom is not so much freedom of volition (in the sense of the old metaphysics) as it is freedom of man as such, man as the embodiment of all humanity, of one man-

1. Friedrich Schiller, 1759–1805, German poet and philosopher.

kind. To recognize in any individual all of humanity is the basic principle of the categorical imperative and the true meaning of freedom. And this ethical principle underlies both Kant's and Schiller's aesthetics, those unique creations of the German spirit, the classical spirit of humanism.

The relationship of aesthetics and ethics is of crucial importance for the aesthetic value of our religious education [with which the first part of this lecture deals]; for the idea of a free mankind is the most significant creation of the prophetic spirit. Messianic man is the man of the one unified mankind. This man of mankind is distinguished and ennobled not by the fact that he is part of a particular nation but solely by his belief in a day when the One God will be acknowledged by the one mankind. From that day on, there will be no strangers among men nor will there be any differences among the tribes of Israel or those of the priests: all nations will be united in one mankind, under One God.

To define man as the embodiment of all mankind is to define the modern concept of man's freedom. Individual freedom is inconceivable without the freedom of mankind. Hence the Hebrew term for freedom signifies both: choosing the good, a capacity given to man; and chosenness of Israel, a concept which, through the development of Messianism, becomes the chosenness of all mankind. "I shall bring the nations to my holy mountain, and make them joyful in my house of prayer, for my house of prayer shall be called the house of prayer for all nations" (Isaiah 56:7).[2]

Such sayings of our Messianism, reflecting an unmistakable and ingrained sense of aesthetics, tend to eliminate the distinction any systematic philosophy must make between ethics and aesthetics. Actually, the ethical profundity of these thoughts is so great and the historical vistas they open so infinite that we are kept from a full appreciation of their aesthetic perfection. The same sense of aesthetics permeates Moses' oratory in the fields of Moab, as related in Deuteronomy. The connection between a free mankind and the free individual is here movingly expressed in the exclamation: "For what great nation is there that hath God so nigh unto them, as the Lord our God is whensoever we call upon Him?" (Deuter-

2. This is a translation of Cohen's rendition of the Biblical text.

onomy 4:7). This nearness of God, characterizing the immediacy of the relationship between God and man or man and God, is not to be understood as merely a symbol of proximity. It is substantively determined, referring to all matters in which "we call upon Him"; and that means those moral concerns which link God and man.[3]

And in the same context it is said that the Torah

> is not in heaven, that thou shouldest say: 'Who shall go up for us to heaven, and bring it unto us, and make us to hear it that we may do it?' Neither is it beyond the sea, that thou shouldest say: 'Who shall go over the sea for us, and bring it unto us, and make us to hear it, that we may do it?' But the word is very nigh unto thee, in thy mouth, and in thy heart, that thou mayest do it (Deuteronomy 30:12–14).

This statement symbolizes man's freedom regarding the law: the Torah is in your mouth and in your heart. The mouth is the instrument of speech, and God is Creator of the fruit of the lips. Thus, speech becomes the vehicle of divine and hence also human reason.

The assertion that the Torah originated in the mind and heart of man is another way of pointing out God's nearness. And if God's nearness is here still proudly referred to as the unique distinction bestowed upon the chosen people, this claim to exclusiveness will be given up as the Messianic idea of One God and one mankind begins to unfold. For now it is felt that all peoples can experience God's nearness because all nations, without exception, are called to be united in one mankind—if only they will acknowledge the One God.

The concept of God's nearness has remained basic to our religion, keeping it free from the raptures and slipperiness of mysticism. And our entire philosophy of religion has made use of the term "God's nearness" (which the psalmist calls "my most precious possession") [4] to describe the highest moral stage man can reach.

3. See "God's Nearness."
4. Psalms 73:28 reads, in the J.P.S. translation: "But as for me, the nearness of God is my good."

Having discussed the ethical principle of a united mankind, let us now examine Judaism's notion of individual man; for when we speak of the aesthetic value of the Jewish concept of man, we think primarily of the individual, that is, of his nature and the unity of his body and soul. This soul within man is, as it were, God within man. "In the image of God created He him" (Genesis 1:27). This could have been said by Plato; and Philo, in fact, actually sees a definite connection between Moses and Plato. The term "image" does not mean likeness, however, for God has neither likeness nor physical form. Image means idea. The idea of man is grounded in the idea of God, with the soul representing the divine element in man's body. "The soul of man is the lamp of the Lord" (Proverbs 20:27).

This Biblical saying sounds the keynote in the approach of our religious philosophy to the question of immortality. And is it not a kind of pantheism when the Psalm, in its profound religiosity, says: "What is man that Thou art mindful of him, and the son of man that Thou rememberest him? Yet Thou hast made him but little lower than a god" (Psalms 8:5,6).[5] Can the concept of man be expressed in more aesthetic terms? And has any other culture produced a religious poetry that, both exalted and naive, simultaneously emphasizes man's frailty and his glory? What is man— and yet, he is a demigod! The sublime and the humorous are here combined, with the sublime giving way to a humble, melancholy acknowledgment of the human condition.

[After citing more examples for the link that exists between religious and aesthetic values in the Bible and in the Lord's prayer, Cohen concludes:]

Aesthetic and religious values then are correlated. For the aesthetic value of our ancient texts is due to their basic religious significance which, in turn, so affects man's emotions that he feels continually driven to express his own religious feelings in new aesthetic forms. . . .

5. This is a translation of Cohen's rendition of the text. The J.P.S. version reads: "What is man, that Thou art mindful of him? And the son of man, that Thou thinkest of him? Yet Tou hast made him but little lower than the angels, . . ."

We cannot truly appreciate the aesthetic value of any work of art without experiencing a sense of reverence for the eternal genius inherent in all creations of abiding aesthetic value. This holds true especially with regard to the Bible, which awakens in us a feeling of reverence for its religious genius and appreciation for its aesthetic sense. As an eminent work of literature, the Bible has infinitely enriched our cultural life by its aesthetics. But beyond this, it has disclosed to us the very ground of our existence insofar as our existence has its roots in our religious ethics, and draws its deepest meaning therefrom.

Trust in God

Popular opinion erroneously regards trust in God as a specifically or even exclusively religious commitment. Actually, though, trust in God is a theoretical prerequisite and indeed an ultimate postulate of ethics as well.

For ethics would remain a system of abstractions concerning man and the potential significance of his existence and accomplishments, were it not for the idea of God which represents at once the foundation and keystone of this theoretical structure and thus firmly secures it.

In ethics the God-idea is man's guarantee that moral postulates are not merely logically valid abstractions but that they have a reality of their own, comparable to that of the logically valid, scientifically sustained notions about nature. True, inasmuch as God cannot be equated with nature nor divine being with the being of the physical world, knowledge of God is not the same as knowledge of nature. But the concepts, as concepts, are comparable even though their subject matter is not. Hence, an analogy between our notions and knowledge of nature and our conception of God is legitimate. Without the God-idea as its terminal point, ethics would remain a maze of concepts. With it, however, we are assured of a guide through this perplexing maze and of the truth behind it. And we are also assured of the eventual realization of the concepts of man and of mankind which ethics has formulated.

What religion refers to as trust, ethics refers to as a cognitive act, an apperception of the idea. Disregarding methodological differences, we see therefore that ethics joins religion in its trust in God as the guarantor of the establishment of morality on earth. Without this guarantee, ethics would be engaged merely in a play of concepts; but where concepts are concerned games are not permissible. The God-idea, however, creates for ethics that objective certainty without which it could not be sure of its own insights. Even though not yet actualized, morality has a reality guaranteed by the God-idea. Thus, ethics does not remain suspended in a state of imperfection, despairing of itself. And morality can compete with the reality of the physical world because and inasmuch as the idea is of the same conceptual origin as any of the notions on which the knowledge of nature is founded.

CHAPTER 5

Religion and Zionism

Editor's Note

Cohen defines Judaism in exclusively religious terms, and in evangelistically religious terms at that. An affirmation of the Jewish religion is an affirmation of the task with which every Jew is charged: to emulate the prophets, God's true emissaries, by proclaiming His truth in word and deed to the world.

"Modern" or "liberal" Judaism emphasizes the universality of its religious tenets and feels this universality is symbolized by Micah's prophecy that Israel shall live dispersed among the nations, "as dew from the Lord." In the midst of these nations, Israel must preserve its distinctiveness. But this distinctiveness is merely a means of preserving and promulgating Judaism's religious ideas, and in no way indicates that the Jew wishes to form a state within the state.

Nor can the "liberal" Jew possibly wish to create a Jewish state in Palestine. The classical concept of Judaism is that of a supranational religion which by definition cannot be tied down to any specific location; above all, it cannot and indeed must not become the religion of a national state. Zionism has an entirely romantic and therefore false notion when it stresses Judaism's national origins rather than its universal goals. Furthermore, Zionism predicates its desire to establish a home for the Jews in Palestine on the erroneous assumption that world Jewry needs a homeland of its own. There are, to be sure, homeless Jews. But homelessness is not a Jewish characteristic, as evidenced by the majority of German Jews who feel thoroughly at home in the country they have every reason to consider their fatherland.

True, Jewish tradition regards Palestine as the "land of our fathers." But Zionism ignores the fact that Palestine is equally the land of our prophets, who perfected our religious ideals and in the process learned to transcend narrow nationalism. The God of the prophet is "the Lord of the whole earth"; and the vision of the prophet is not that of a particular state but of the Messianic future. "And it is," says Cohen, "this future alone which we acknowledge as our true home."

An Argument Against Zionism

A REPLY TO DR. MARTIN BUBER'S OPEN LETTER TO HERMANN COHEN

The Jewish question is not limited to a geographically or socio-politically isolated people. It concerns a people that lives dispersed among other nations and must therefore establish as well as clarify its socio-political relationship to each of them individually. . . .

The state, in our view, is the very hub of all culture. In fact, even man's "I" remains an empirically ambiguous concept as long as it is not objectified by his identification with the body politic. I achieve true self-identification only to the extent to which I become part of my nation's ideal personality. All our emotions are concentrated in our commitment to our country.

The question, for us, is therefore no longer whether to give priority to science or to religion among our cultural interests. For the state is the focal point of them all, and all cultural questions are determined from this point alone. The idea of the state, however, culminates in the postulate for a federation of nations and thus becomes the quintessence of ethics. The realization of morality on earth must, consequently, be brought about by the state as the symbol of a federation of nations.

Hence, we are not faced with a conflict between state and religion or between state and science [on which, according to Cohen, all ethics must be based [1]]. Our ancient Jewish philosophers liber-

1. See "The Social Ideal as Seen by Plato and by the Prophets."

ated us from this nightmare of other religions by making knowledge the prime requisite of religion.

Our religion, then, ascribes the same function to the state as does ethics. Nevertheless, Judaism and the Jewish people experience a difficulty inherent in the problem of the modern state which wishes to be a national state. For insofar as they constitute a distinct ethnic group, the Jews seem to form a state within such a state.

In the face of this modern difficulty the more liberal Jews of all countries exclaim, without prior agreement, in their self-defense: "Insofar as the modern state is a national state, we neither wish to form a state within the state, nor do we wish to be a distinct nation. But ours is and remains a distinct religion; and for the preservation of this religion of ours we are and remain, as a matter of principle, a distinct ethnic group, a distinct nationality."

Can one ethicize nationality, that "natural fact," with a weightier argument than that it is the historical vehicle needed for the preservation of religion? All the emotional factors my opponent emphasizes in favor of a Jewish nation apply equally to our concept of a religious nationality which we see as the historical factor of religion.

But having made this point, which actually should unify us, I now contend—and in the main I speak for all modern Jews—that religion is a factor of history but not its philosophical point of reference. How does the Jewish religion, empirically conditioned and burdened as it is, view the basic ethical principle of the state?

Whatever Judaism and its adherents have suffered externally and internally has its origin in this question. The nations in their blindness say: "There must be no groups among us which, for whatever fictitious reasons, enjoy any state-like, separate existence." And the Jews, hard-pressed by the ambivalences of modern life and the anxieties of our day, and thus inclined to leave their faith, say: "There is an irreconcilable conflict between the Jewish religion and the foundation of modern national life, the national state. Our commitment to the state, therefore, requires us to break with Judaism."

But modern Judaism counters such fallacies with the thesis that it is solely and exclusively our religion which sets us apart from our state, hence also from our nation.

Dare one still assert that this thesis is nothing but an embarrassed subterfuge, or, worse yet, that it shows a cowardly tendency towards assimilation? Such an assertion would do a serious injustice to our conviction that we have an ethical obligation to the modern state. Moreover, we feel that anyone doubting this ethical obligation should not even wish to be part of a modern state. It is wrong and also misleading to claim all ideal and historical motives and their concomitant emotions for our Jewish consciousness, and then to maintain that one has no moral energies of heart or mind left for our national-political consciousness. Zionism mercilessly disposes of us liberal Jews by declaring us deluded for feeling at home in the civilized countries in which we are living. Our so-called delusions are contrasted with the general homelessness of the Jewish people. And this homeless Jewish people alone is supposed to represent Jewish reality. We, however, who are regarded as Jews in name only, are—justifiably, it is felt—read out of the Jewish people.

Zionism thus tailors Jewish reality to fit its own preconceived notions. And Jewish reality is circumscribed ever more narrowly: only in Palestine and only in a Jewish state can a "silted-over," a "fictitious" Judaism be extricated from the undesirable accretions of diaspora-existence. The entire history of Judaism is here ideologically distorted. Ghetto mentality is not seen as a specter of Judaism but as its true spirit, or as the spirit of true Judaism. All cultural endeavors of Jewish history are condemned as illusory, belabored abstractions having nothing to do with authentic Judaism. And our modern liberal movement is regarded as but a continuation of those earlier illusions which must now be overcome.

The problems and predicaments, let alone conflicts, of modern cultural life do not exist for this narrow nationalism. Here, the Jew is a Jew only insofar as he is conscious of his Jewish nationality. But what if a Jew who affirms his Jewish nationality feels destined, or finds it incumbent upon himself also to affirm his German nationality? Would that really be merely an error, an illusion, a political abstraction? Or does the modern Jew's actual participation in the life of the state to which he has in freedom pledged his allegiance not require also that he attempt an inner integration of the two forces which motivate him—a vital and constructive concern for the country of which he is a citizen, and a full affirmation of his own past history—so that his German and his Jewish consciousness are fused into one? Or has the modern Jew's sense of dual nationality no need of unification?

In the face of that ruthlessness with which the entire existing reality of Judaism—already delineated by Jeremiah—is being rejected, all of us liberal Jews maintain, with the assurance of our historical instinct: no restriction of civil rights must be allowed to make us waver in our sense of obligation and total commitment to the country we claim as our own. To us liberal Jews, the state represents more than merely one of many cultural phenomena to be subsumed under our religion. Even our ancestors in Arab Spain, in whose cultural milieu they flourished, were hardly that limited in their thinking. And in the meantime, we have become fully aware of the blessings the modern state has bestowed upon us by letting us participate in its intellectual life and in all the ever-changing manifestations of its national spirit. Our horizons have grown wider. We apply to our religion the control of our ethics and scientific philosophy, that true center of all culture. Even our ancient sages were already approaching this methodological procedure; yet they were and remained loyal to their religion. And that holds equally true for us.

Is my opponent's contention that there are only two ways open to authentic Judaism—either absolute Orthodoxy or Zionism—truly commensurate with the reality of our history? Are all the other roads and directions our history has taken really nothing but devious paths that necessarily lead to degeneration? And what is the criterion by which to decide whether the road to Palestine alone will determine the true shape of our future? It seems obvious that our religion itself must serve as the criterion by which to judge the authenticity and character of the totality of Jewish existence.

Modern Judaism is history-oriented; it derives its sense of self-identity from its historical development. And this development was given its inner direction by prophetism and its lofty concept of a Messianic mankind.

We interpret our entire history as pointing to this Messianic goal. Thus, we see the destruction of the Jewish state as an exemplification of the theodicy of history. The same Micah who said that God requires man to do justly also conceived of the providential metaphor: "And the remnant of Jacob shall be in the midst of many peoples, as dew from the Lord" (Micah 5:6). We are proudly aware of the fact that we continue to live as divine dew among the nations; we wish to remain among them and be a creative force for them. All our prophets have us living among the nations, and all view "Israel's remnant" from the perspective of its world mission. And it is from that perspective alone that the natural desire of the remnant to return to the land of its origin must be understood. For hardly ever is it stated that the remnant is to return all by itself. There is almost always a reference to "many" or to "all peoples" which will be flocking to the light of God; and the prophets felt that they themselves had been chosen to bring this light to all nations.

Our modern Judaism represents this religion of mankind. And the awareness of this religio-cultural goal of ours prevents us from feeling any possible conflict between our Judaism and our Germanism. But the Jews of all other countries may, by dint of their religion, feel equally free of similar conflicts. For the Jewish religion, thanks to its God-concept, is an entirely universal religion. Nothing can vitiate this Messianic faith of ours—no historical reality, no destitution, not even the happiness that has come to us with our attainment of civil rights. "Happy is he that waiteth (Daniel 12:12): Messianic hope alone guarantees our "reality," our authentic existence.

Hope and confidence also provide the basis for our political orientation. We love Germany and all it stands for not merely because we love our homeland as the bird loves its nest; nor do we love it merely because we draw our spiritual sustenance largely from the treasure-troves of the German mind (and surely not from the Bible or Talmud alone). Weighty though these motivations for our love may be, they lose some of their significance when compared to our awareness of that innermost accord existing between the German spirit and our Messianic religiosity. The German spirit is the spirit of classical humanism and true universalism.[2]

[After an admiring enumeration of German poets and thinkers, Cohen continues:]

What other people possesses such unity of classical poetry and philosophy! All these German thinkers are prophets of the one humanity. Therefore it is only natural that we German Jews should feel at one with ourselves, as Jews and as Germans. And the Jews of other countries, whose religious life has been fructified by the science of Judaism (which has its roots in Germany), should learn to acknowledge and appreciate Germany's central significance for moral culture; they can surely do so without doing violence to their own national loyalties. They ought to consider it their cultural task, moreover, despite all the political jealousy and envy that bedevil us today, to implant this attitude in the peoples among whom they live.

This politico-religious orientation of ours constitutes, for all practical purposes, the difference between us and Zionism. While the Zionist believes that Judaism can be preserved only by an all-encompassing Jewish nationalism, we are of the opposite view, believing that only a universal, mankind-oriented Judaism can preserve the Jewish religion. An understanding of this difference—which is by no means merely one of tactics—might serve to explain or even excuse the bitterness of our conflict. Both parties, I grant, are fervently concerned with our religious survival. To ensure this survival, I certainly and unconditionally ask for the preservation of our nationality [that is, our ethnic group-distinctiveness]. But at the same time, and equally unconditionally, I ask for our political integration into the modern national state. For our political integration is the prerequisite as well as the guarantee of our religious survival. . . .

Palestine is not merely the land of our fathers; it is the land of our prophets, who established and perfected the ideal of our religion. Hence, we consider it indeed the Holy Land, though only in the sense that our timeless, sacred heritage originated there. But

2. See "Affinities Between the Philosophy of Kant and Judaism"; also: "The German and the Jewish Ethos."

by the same token by which we regard our religious present as a projection of the future we regard the moral world as it unfolds throughout history as our real Promised Land.

And here, if anywhere, lies the essential difference between Jewish classicism and romanticism. The classical concept of our religion points towards the future of mankind, and not towards the past of an ethnic community whose holiness, rather than being tied down to a geographical location, is bound up with its world-historical idea. For us as for the psalmist, God dwells in Israel's songs of praise (Psalms 22:4). These, however, cannot ring out into the world by themselves. It is up to us to remain God's true emissaries spreading these songs, in their unique distinctiveness, throughout the world. . . .

Our understanding of the concept of a Messianic future is not expressed by that metaphor which has the Lord prepare a meal on Mount Zion for all the nations. Instead, we invoke all those Biblical utterances which proclaim, without resorting to imagery, the One God as "the Lord of the whole earth" (Micah 4:13). We therefore see the entire historical world as the future abode of our religion. And it is this future alone which we acknowledge as our true home.

Religion and Zionism

When Zionism insists on referring to the "publicly recognized, legally secured home" [1] it wishes to establish for the Jews, without adding the qualification "for those Jews who are in need of such a home," I fail to see that this movement pursues a policy of truth. Instead, I consider its slogan an insult to the patriotism of those Jews who feel, politically as well as emotionally, at home in their fatherland. And by the very ambiguity of this motto Zionism becomes for me an utterly incomprehensible untruth.

1. First Zionist Congress, Basle, 1897.

Yet man's truthfulness is the indispensable foundation of his personal religion. Jewish wisdom even makes truth the "seal" of God's divinity. If, therefore, man's political orientation implies a violation of the truth, his religious orientation becomes suspect too.

The distinguishing mark of the Jewish religion is its idea of the One God with its corollary, the one Messianic mankind. With this concept of the one mankind which will acknowledge the One God, Israel's prophets destroy paganism. And they see in the message of one mankind—which the Jewish people is meant to bring to the nations of the world—the reason for Israel's chosenness.

Yet Zionist literature (including the writings of German rabbis) abounds in frivolous derisions of this supreme idea of the Jewish religion, an idea it demeans by calling it a product of the sentimental humanitarianism of liberal rationalism.

This difference in religious orientation alone suffices to set up a dividing wall between our Messianic Judaism and Zionism. If, nevertheless, a timid attempt at mediation and reconciliation is being made, one ought to take care not to belittle the importance of the Messianic God-idea. For we cannot conceive of a Judaism devoid of hope for a Messianic mankind. And we feel that those who think Judaism and its basic teachings are as a matter of principle reserved for the Jewish people alone deny the One God of Messianic mankind. We regard Israel's chosenness solely as history's means to accomplish the divine chosenness of mankind.

The Talmud tells of a man who is led before the divine judge and interrogated only in matters pertaining to his moral conduct, except for this one additional question: "And did you hope for redemption?" This story demonstrates clearly the profound significance of the concept of Messianic hope to the Jew, and how deeply it has always been ingrained in his religious consciousness.

CHAPTER 6

German Humanism and Jewish Messianism

Editor's Note

Cohen's Jewish religiosity is almost matched in depth and fervor by what might be called his German religiosity. In fact, the two complement each other, resulting in his earnestly held and rhapsodically voiced conviction that the synthesis between German humanism and Jewish Messianism, exemplified by the Jewish Reform Movement in Germany, represents the most mature stage yet of mankind's ethico-cultural development.

There is, he asserts, a profound and genuinely spiritual kinship between the German and the Jewish ethos. Germany's neo-humanistic ideals, propounded in her philosophy and literature during the late eighteenth and early nineteenth centuries, are in full accord with the Messianic ideals of prophetic Judaism. What is more, Jewish Messianism—whose ideological significance a ghettoized Jewry had not been able to appreciate fully—was revitalized by the writings of idealistic German poets and thinkers, and thus underwent a true renascence.

In contradistinction to the age of Voltaire in France, German Enlightenment regards religion as an important means for the advancement of the "idea of morality," a goal common to both German Protestantism and Judaism. The notion of one mankind, understood as a human and humane brotherhood which must one day extend across all artificial barriers that separate individuals and nations, is as basic to Kantian as to prophetic ethics. There is, moreover, a definite relationship between the monotheistic principle of divine Oneness and the principles of idealistic philosophy. And it is Cohen's contention that German idealism and Hebrew prophetism alike derive their sense of world-history from a conviction that the life of individuals and nations has meaning and pur-

175

pose, and that man is innately able and spiritually destined to achieve the good if only he will earnestly seek it.

The German Jew is part of his nation's "ideal personality" and his commitment to his country must be total and twofold, for Germany is both his political fatherland and his cultural motherland. And since German and Jewish ethical ideals are well nigh identical, Germany constitutes the Jew's religious home too. In fact, the scholarship of German Protestantism has created an intellectual and spiritual atmosphere so conducive to the development of religious thought that the German Jew might easily make the preservation of his own religion a mandate of the German state.

But though Cohen confesses to "a sense of the closest religious communion" between himself and Germany, a feeling which flows "from the accord that exists between Jewish Messianism and German humanism," his heart and mind remain open to the plight of Jews in other countries. When Germany considers closing her borders to the Jews of Eastern Europe during World War I, Cohen argues publicly, on religious and humanitarian grounds, in favor of their admission.

During the same period, he pleads with the Jews of America to remember the cultural debt they owe Germany. Most of them, he asserts, have some inner tie to the latter, whose intellectual climate has favored the restructuring of the Jewish religion from within and whose spiritual ethos, so closely akin to Judaism's, has in some measure contributed, directly or indirectly, to their own religious and cultural development.

The German and the Jewish Ethos I

With the advent of the Reformation, modern man began to realize that human insights can lead to two different kinds of certitude: that of the exact sciences and that of faith. Though necessarily outside the realm of science, questions of faith were not, however, dealt with in a spirit of skepticism. Instead, they were compiled and retained as an ethics which now took its place alongside religion. Far from being regarded as a competitor of or replacement for religion, ethics was seen as its support and guarantee or, so to speak, as the idea of religion.

This attitude reflects the difference between the German Enlightenment and the age of Voltaire and the Encyclopedists. The German Enlightenment does not view religion as an infamy that ought to be eradicated but rather as a means by which mankind attempted, on whatever level of its development, to bring about the realization of the idea of morality.

It was, however, only when Protestantism drew a distinction between the two kinds of intellectual certitude that the scientifically oriented conscience of the modern world felt really reassured. In fact, the inner development of both religion and ethics is due to this exposition of cultural idealism. Unless he distinguishes moral —hence also religious—certitude from that of science, modern man possesses neither intellectual honesty nor personal integrity.

Quite unintentionally, we touch here already upon a connection between cultural idealism and the Bible or Judaism. Let us therefore examine the fundamental principles constituting Judaism's religious distinctiveness.

Though Biblical Judaism does not anticipate philosophical idealism in any scientific way, its orientation towards philosophical speculation is unmistakable. God reveals Himself as He who is: "I am that I am" (Exodus 3:14). In these words (using the future tense), the One God reveals Himself from the midst of the burning bush. Oneness now becomes the distinguishing mark of God's being. God's Oneness means that His being is the One and Only being; that except for divine being, there is no real being; or that all other being is mere appearance, as Plato would say. God, however, is being as such,[1] and in Him the world, particularly the world of man, has its ground and foundation. But this God is beyond all sense-perception, beyond all image and likeness. He—somewhat like the idea—can only be "purely intuited," can only be thought.

1. See "Uniqueness Rather Than Unity of God."

To think of God is to think in the manner not of science but of love. Knowledge of God is love. "Love" is the true Biblical term for what the religious language of the Reformation refers to as "faith." The Greeks, and Plato with them, felt similarly that Eros represented the ultimate, the most inward degree of knowledge.

It was inevitable that Judaism, with its definition of knowledge of God as love, should, once it had come into contact with the Greek spirit, realize its own kinship to idealism and seek to make use of Greek concepts in formulating its own thought. And what Philo started—perhaps not entirely originally—was elaborated upon in later centuries. In the ninth century, Jewish thinking begins to give its religious concepts a philosophical form. Moses Maimonides, the twelfth-century luminary, becomes central to this movement. The great scholastics draw upon his thought; his theory of the divine attributes and thus of the problem of divine being serves as a model for Cusanus; and Leibniz too epitomizes Maimonides' writings.

Maimonides exemplifies the spirit of Protestantism in medieval Judaism. Though nowhere attacking religious institutions, he seeks everywhere to detect the underlying reasons for their existence. He obviously feels that these institutions are in need of rational argumentation; they are, in fact, viable and of continued value only to the extent to which they lend themselves to such rational argumentation. He himself undergirds his religious idealism with a general scientific rationalism. But where Maimonides' philosophy goes to the very root meaning of the God-concept, it reflects a genuine Platonic idealism in his definition of God as the only real mode of being and the only originator of all existence.

If God's Oneness is the first fundamental concept of Judaism, the purity of man's soul is the second. The Jew prays every morning: "Oh my God, the soul which Thou gavest me is pure; Thou didst create it, Thou didst form it, Thou didst breathe it into me; and Thou wilt take it from me, but wilt restore it to me hereafter." This notion is absolutely basic to Jewish religiosity. Therefore no Holy Ghost nor any other mediator can come between God and man. "The mediator between God and man is man's reason." This is a pronouncement by Ibn Ezra,[2] the highly important first critic of the Bible. The holy spirit is just as much the spirit of man as it is the spirit of God. The holy God has imbued man with His spirit. Therefore the human spirit is a holy spirit.[3]

Judaism's concept of man's reconciliation with God and his redemption from sin is based on the idea of the purity of his soul and the holiness of his spirit. Though man may have defiled it, his soul can never lose its original purity if only he will go about the work of his redemption in the right way. If he seeks his exculpation through serious repentance, filled with remorse and in a spirit of genuine contrition yet absolute trust, his sin and its burden will be taken from his soul.[4]

After David has committed the greatest sin of his life, the psalmist has him say: "Cast me not away from Thy presence, and take not Thy holy spirit from me" (Psalms 51:13). Except for a double passage in Isaiah which is less telling, this passage is the only one in the Old Testament that makes mention of the holy spirit. This concept is introduced here so as to redeem man from his anxiety and from the fear that his sin might rob him of his soul's purity. Judaism's concept of the soul, then, assures man of his redemption by God. And consonant with this idealistic view of his soul and spirit is the thought that man's religious salvation depends on his own moral effort.

Now, it might appear as if this fundamental idealistic principle were incompatible with another basic concept of Judaism, the concept of law (which has been under attack ever since Paul). But if we remember that the two notions of autonomy and universal law —the two poles, as it were, representing freedom and duty—go together in Kant's ethics too, we recognize in this innermost sanctum of the German spirit an innermost affinity to the spirit of Judaism.[5] Here, God's commandment constitutes man's duty. And this sense of a divinely commanded duty together with a sense of

2. Abraham ibn Ezra (1092–1167), Jewish Bible exegete and poet in Spain.
3. See "The Holy Spirit."
4. See "The Concept of Reconciliation" and "The Day of Atonement."
5. See "Affinities Between the Philosophy of Kant and Judaism."

reverence will, according to Jewish religious thought, lead to a freely rendered service of love, that is, love of God through love of man. . . .

The idea of mankind is basic to Kant's ethics. With it, he frees the moral concept of man from all the sensualism, eudaemonism [6] and egotism of empirical man. Thus, the categorical imperative, as postulate for mankind, can be definitively formulated in this way: "Do not act as an I, in the empirical sense, but as the I of mankind, in the ideal sense. Regard your own person as well as any other not in the physical, racial, or narrowly historical terms of individual existence, but exclusively as an embodiment of the eternal, world-historical idea of mankind." Mankind is man's final purpose and goal. And the individual, being an end-in-himself, must therefore never become a "mere means" for other men. This idea of mankind gave rise to the development of socialism. For mankind is the principle of all that is human—in the individual, the state, and world history. . . .

[There is, says Cohen, a difference between the idea of mankind postulated by German idealism and the concept of *humanité* advanced by the French Revolution. He contends that only the German concept has an ethical foundation.]

Here, it is manifest once again how much Germanism and Judaism have in common. For the German idea of mankind has its origin in the Messianism of Israel's prophets, whose spirit doubtlessly affected German humanism profoundly. And prophetic Messianism must be seen as the keystone of Judaism, its crown as well as its root. Moreover, Messianism furnishes the creative and basic motive for monotheism and is its ultimate consequence.

It is true that Messianism from the very outset, nevertheless, is indicative of both a sense of national politics and national religiosity, for the people's national and religious spirit have a common source. By pointing to a Messianic future, the prophets intend both to improve their people morally and heal it politically; to frighten it with threats of extinction and console it with promises of restoration and redemption. And later, too, religious consciousness remains fixed upon that special task of the Messiah, the final

6. See footnote, p. 79.

redemption of the Jew from bloody persecutions, from the constant torture of being shunted from place to place, and (more urgently still) from the constant denigration of his religious honor, the honor of his sacred faith.

Yet in spite of all of this, the world-historical perspective of Messianism was never completely obscured for the Jew; his prayer kept the Messianic ideal before him and made it come alive. On the main festivals of the Jewish year dedicated to man's reconciliation with God, the Messianic hope also provides, as it were, a guide-post for the individual in need of comfort and seeking redemption from sin. He is uplifted by the promise of a united mankind: "so that all peoples may be united by one bond"—this is the prayer of Rosh Hashanah and Yom Kippur, days of reconciliation for all nations as well as for the individual.

Thus, our medieval philosophers of religion continued, though with certain individual modifications, to regard Messianism as a fundamental concept of Judaism. There is a statement made in the ninth [7] century by Saadyah Gaon [8] which has not lost its relevance even in the twentieth century: "Our nation is a nation only by dint of its teachings." And the interpretation of the daily prayer: "He remembereth the covenant of the fathers" by one of the strictest ritualists of the sixteenth century, Moses Isserles of Cracow, is equally significant. He points out that the prayer avoids speaking of a covenant of *our* fathers so that all men may feel included in this covenant with God. This idea was voiced during the most difficult times of persecution, and thus amply demonstrates that the Jew never lost sight of the Messianic principle.

Nevertheless, it is understandable that during those days of the universal ghetto this fundamental prophetic concept with its central importance to the Jewish religion did not play a vital role in the individual's life though it did sustain the mood of his prayers. Moreover, Christianity had made use of the idea of the Messiah in a way that denied the Jew his right to exist as a Jew. The Messiah was supposed to have already come, with his second coming all

---

7. An error in the original (*Juedische Schriften,* Vol. II, p. 265); should read: tenth century.
8. See footnote, p. 77.

that could be hoped for, and with the nations, through their belief in Christ, already united in their belief in God. . . .

Thus it can be seen why, during this entire period, Messianism, as a dogma, paled into insignificance when compared to Judaism's other ethical ideas. Though the Jew of the Enlightenment continued to express daily—in the magnificent words of the concluding prayer, the *Alenu*—his hope for a time when all idolatry would disappear and the kingdom of the Almighty would be established upon the earth, the universal kingdom of religion had actually become somewhat galling to his taste.

And this may help explain the strange fact that neither in Mendelssohn's [9] own writings nor in those of his followers and disciples is Messianism emphasized as a basic Jewish tenet. During Mendelssohn's lifetime, Messianism as an ethico-cultural concept was not a relevant factor in the personal religiosity of the Jew. So far, at least, I have found no evidence to the contrary in the literature of that time. . . .

Hence, Mendelssohn's own philosophy of history recognizes no steady progress in the world. It would indeed seem then that the religio-ethical horizon of the Jew was somewhat obstructed during this period, owing to a development which, however natural, is regrettable in a people professing this particular faith. They had temporarily lost sight of what had once been their very own: the concept of the Messiah as the Messiah of the world. Such was the narrowing and obscuring effect the ghetto had upon their outlook, along with their continual fear of persecution.

Eventually, however, the Jew saw his Messianic idea revitalized in and through the German spirit. For Herder [10] ushered in the dawn of a new humanity so that the Messiah of the prophets, that most unique possession of the Jew, was restored to him in the idealistic postulate of German ethics, a united mankind.

Presently, the German sermon took up this idea. First Saals-

9. Moses Mendelssohn, (1729–1786; Germany), whose enlightened philosophy and translation of the Hebrew Bible into German were largely responsible for the intellectual emancipation of Central European Jewry.
10. Johann Gottfried Herder (1744–1803); German philosopher and scholar.

chuetz [11] and then especially the young Abraham Geiger, whose
entire thought and work were based on this notion, once again
proclaimed Judaism as a world religion.

Now we can understand the impact Mendelssohn had upon
German Judaism, not so much as a Jew who believed in Messianism but as a German whose thought was closely akin to German
humanism and German ethics. And now we can understand, too,
why German Judaism has exerted and continues to exert such a
profound influence on the Jews of all other countries. . . .

I believe that the Jews of France, England, and Russia owe a
debt of filial piety to Germany, for it is the motherland of their
soul to the extent that their religion constitutes their soul.

In these epoch-making times, so fateful for all nations, we as
Jews are proud to be Germans. And we are aware of our task to
convince our coreligionists the world over of the religious import
of the German ethos and of its influence as well as its claim on the
Jews of all nations: its influence, that is, on their religious development and on all their cultural endeavors. We know that we as
German Jews share in a central cultural force destined to unite all
nations in the spirit of a Messianic mankind. Hence we feel justified in rejecting the accusation that we have throughout history
been an element of decomposition among peoples and nations.
When circumstances once again permit man to engage in a serious
search for international understanding and world-wide peace, our
example may well serve as a model for those willing to acknowledge the preeminence of the German mind in all intellectual and
spiritual matters. But as long as this good will is lacking everywhere, we do not think it possible to establish an adequate basis
for any genuine international understanding. . . .

[Our political reality is still deplorably far from our goal. Yet]
the concept of a unified mankind must serve as ethical lodestar
for the inner development of all nations and all moral individuals.
[True, before we can have a unified mankind, we must be organized in states. However,] the idea of the state culminates in a
federation of nations. . . . The German ethos must become the

11. Joseph Lewin Saalschuetz (1801–1863); archeologist, preacher, and
teacher of religion in Koenigsberg, Germany.

central force of such a federation which will establish world peace and with it the foundation for a world of true culture. A just war is the preparation for perpetual peace. . . .

The kindred spirit linking Germanism and Judaism is thus focused on the most distant point of the world's historical horizon; and the lodestar guiding man's progress to perpetual peace is the Messianic idea of Israel's prophetism, that quintessence of the Jewish religion.

As they themselves hope for the Messianic age, the prophets make hope the basic affect of politics, history, and religion. What others refer to as faith, they refer to as hope. This turning away from the actually given, this forward-thrust of the present into the future, this liberation of man's mind from the overpowering grip of reality—all of this constitutes their idealism. Prophetic idealism is therefore not inferior in degree or extent to the idealism with which philosophy views all being. Indeed, the prophets' hope and vision of the future encompass not only the world of man but even that of nature.

Yet if one were to ask them: "How do you justify your faith in the future of mankind?" they would answer in their simple way: "The One God, the Creator of the earth and the generations of man, has implanted His holy spirit into man. And inherent in that spirit of holiness is the guarantee that mankind was created to pursue an eternally valid moral goal." God's purpose guarantees mankind's purpose. The prophets cannot give us any other rationale. For them there is actually no better rationale than that conceived by mankind in the eternal, boundless idea of the One God.

German ethics has conceived of a theoretically more adequate validation for this belief and has thus renewed that guarantee. But both German ethics and Jewish religiosity have their foundation in God, that "mighty fortress," and neither need nor desire any other anchorage.

The German and the Jewish Ethos II

If it is to be conceded that German Jewry should maintain its ethnic cohesion, it must also be stated, and in unequivocal terms, that such a perpetuation of Jewish group distinction is to serve merely as a means to preserve the purity of the Jewish faith. There must not be the slightest doubt, however, as to the ultimate hope and fundamental principle of this faith, a principle that restores ancient Judaism to new life within modern Judaism: the concept of the Messianic future in which a united mankind will acknowledge the One and Only God. This concept is the epitome of monotheism and represents the root strength of the Jewish religion—which, because of its Messianic goal, cannot be a state religion. This is the meaning we German Jews see in the destruction of the Jewish state (already predicted by the prophets), and this is the meaning we see in our entire history, which we read as the history of our religion.

This quintessence of our living religiosity must not be diluted; nor must Judaism's final goal be rendered dubious by a policy which no persecution of Jews and no compassion with Jewish destitution can justify. For such a policy is contrary to our religious teachings: already Jeremiah admonishes the exiled Jews to concern themselves exclusively with the welfare of the country in which they live (Jeremiah 29:4–7).

I cannot see how my commitment to my own religious group could possibly imply a commitment to a country other than my own. As religion demands man's whole, undivided heart, so does the state. I must leave it to my own country to bring about, within the profusion of its other moral goals, the realization of my endeavors and hopes for my religion and its followers all over the world. All my political endeavors and hopes, however, are completely bound up with this country of mine. It is undoubtedly my right and even my duty as a religious individual, let alone as a professing Jew, to charge my German fatherland with the ideal task of protecting and preserving the Jewish group so that the religion of the One and Only God may be preserved. But I do not see how a German citizen can combine his natural concern for the preservation of Judaism with any desire to promote the establishment of a Jewish state, without falling short of fulfilling his ideal duties towards the German state—namely, to adhere to it alone, with an undivided heart, enthusiasm, and complete trust.

By saying this I do not at all accuse any particular party—which need not even exist as far as this discussion of principle is concerned. But I feel it is my patriotic as well as religious duty to sound a warning against certain views and voice my objections to them. Despite many odds, the German Jew is convinced of his right to preserve and perpetuate the distinctiveness of the Jewish religion in his fatherland and subsequently in all civilized countries. This conviction of ours must not be mistaken for double loyalty, however. Not only does it represent no threat to or infringement upon our patriotism: it even motivates us to make the preservation of our religion a religious and cultural mandate of the German state.

Any study of the past development of religion and any contemplation of its future will convince modern man that it is incumbent upon the cultural forces of the world and their leading spirit, Germany, to promulgate the idea of Israelite monotheism. The originality of Israel's God-concept alone makes its further preservation and elaboration imperative for the historical-minded. For there is an inner connection between the originality with which the monotheistic principle was conceived and formulated, and the fact that it remained unadorned and free from all additional notions that later came into play. Yet however intimately linked the concepts of God and man may be in all cultures, if the monotheistic principle in its original meaning for all being and all existence is to be maintained, it is absolutely mandatory that we think of it in strictly unitary terms. God's Oneness is of fundamental significance for all being, constituting the unique value of an uncompromising monotheism with which we therefore cannot ever dispense.

Furthermore, there is a definite relationship between the concept of divine Oneness and the principles of idealism. And if this assertion is correct—as should be evidenced by the history of philosophy alone—it follows that the preservation of a pure and absolute monotheism is indispensable even for the preservation of idealism. For it is not pantheism, for which all being is comprised in God, that has been proven right, but rather monotheism, with all being derived from and grounded in God. And this grounding of all being in God is predicated, in turn, upon God's unity.

Hence, an ever more candid acknowledgment and an ever deeper appreciation of the value of Israelite monotheism for an idealistic world-view would seem to be a theoretical prerequisite for a profound and genuine understanding between Germanism and Judaism. And with an increasing awareness in the ranks of general scholarship of the need to study the Old Testament scientifically, it will be realized how good it is that there are still people in the world, and in our dear Germany at that, who believe simply in the One God, a concept free of any added divine or human elements or secondary meanings. . . .

We German Jews find ourselves in a singularly favorable position (as we have shown elsewhere)[1]: we can see for ourselves and can recognize as an incontestable historical fact the great impact the German spirit has had not only on our intellectual life but also on our religious spirit and on the scientific study of Judaism. And we realize that the German Jews, in turn, have exerted an almost exclusive influence on the Jews of all modern nations—on their religious ideas, their rituals, and their involvement in the science of Judaism. And as for our spiritual life, we derive a sense of the closest religious communion from the accord existing between Jewish Messianism and German humanism. Our feeling for Germany and its people has therefore religious overtones, so to speak, and is marked by a sense of religious affirmation. In perfect equa-

1. See "The German and the Jewish Ethos I" and: "Thou Shalt Not Go About as a Slanderer."

nimity and harmony of soul, we feel as secure in our German patriotism as in our Jewish religion, whose root and crown are the One God of one mankind. And our alleged Jewish particularism, excepting general motives of compassion and charity for our persecuted coreligionists, is limited to our duty to preserve our faith. But seen under the higher aspect of religion, justice, and humanitarianism, this duty should actually be regarded as a universal cultural task.

[True, some Germans still mistrust Jews. Nevertheless, and despite frequent disappointments and misunderstanding, we must not lose confidence that the true German spirit will continue to pursue the highest ethical goals.]

To ensure the ethical conduct of its religious and public affairs, Germany must realize that nothing will endanger and corrupt a people more than its attempt to play providence even with regard to politics. No political self-interest, neither immediate nor long-range, entitles a people to decide whether another people or nationality has the right to live. And if this is true in the realm of politics, it is equally true in the realm of religion.

The survival of the Jew is, in any event, probably the most amazing phenomenon in the entire history of the world. And if humility in the face of history is indeed a virtue, it is nowhere more called-for than with regard to those remnants of an ancient past who have not merely survived physically but are undeniably engaged in cultural pursuits. There has never been a dearth of German individuals who have been fond of and have put their trust in their German Jews. Maybe—who can foretell the course of history?—it will one day be considered not among the least of its glories that Germany did not only grant protective and civil rights to its Jews, but that it also made them part of that spirit which informs German science, German art, and all other expressions of German creativity; that it lent its most sympathetic support to the cultivation of the Jewish religion to the benefit of the entire world; and that it paved the way for the attainment of a spiritual harmony between German and Jew on a level probably unmatched in the modern world—a harmony for which the Jew, to be sure, owes the greater debt of gratitude.

Assuming that the basic premises of the foregoing reflections are not entirely incorrect, we might then come to this conclusion: by promoting the welfare of German Jewry, the German people, imbued with its special spirit, has made a most valuable contribution to the inner development not only of Judaism but of religion as such.

On Closing the Borders

I know I must not state my views and wishes concerning the political problem I shall here discuss without taking a searching look at my responsibilities as a German. And I also know full well that I must take into account my German coreligionists' eagerness to accept their responsibilities as citizens, while trying to understand why their stand on the question under discussion differs from my own. I am quite aware—and make no secret of the fact—that my objection to any plan to close our borders to the Jews of Eastern Europe is influenced by my religious outlook. This religious outlook of mine is primarily an ethical outlook, however. For to me, the ideal of any constitutional state must be a united mankind. Kant once said that the earth has a spherical surface lest any man have more of a claim than another to any specific spot on it. Thus, even the political deliberations of any particular state ought to be guided by the ideal image of a universal state.

This principle of ethics and its postulate of a world-wide community of nations are consonant with a fundamental principle of Jewish theology: the One God "loves the stranger." This concept of God's love for the stranger gave rise to the commandment, addressed to Israel, to "love the stranger." And from this commandment to love the stranger emerged the commandment to love man as such, to love one's fellow man.

It is the duty of any government both from an ethical and religious point of view to grant protection to the stranger oppressed in his own country. Probably no political measure ever taken by England has so enhanced its standing among the nations as its introduction of the right of political asylum (though this act might quite possibly lead to conflicts with other countries).

It would be a meaningful by-product of this war [1] if our fatherland were also to acknowledge and share in the international obligation to extend protective rights to the foreigner in need of them. I have already expressed my hope elsewhere that Germany will recognize what I consider to be its mission. And I have repeatedly raised my voice in these great yet difficult times on behalf of my East European coreligionists—a task made mandatory by my position as a scholar, by my age, and my experience.

The experiences of a long life have created a close relationship between me, the German born in Anhalt, and these people of Eastern Europe. I have revered some of them as my Talmud teachers and I gratefully remember nearly all of them. I have come to know, among these men, the character traits of the unworldly sage, the unselfish sufferer, and the pure idealist in all matters of mind and morals. And they have, throughout my life, claimed my admiration both for their intellectual acumen and depth and their moral stature and selfless renunciation of the world. The single-minded assiduousness alone with which these men pursue their Talmudic studies provides us with a personal example for all scholarly work.

And these East European Jews combine intellectual energy with religious enthusiasm. Though this combination is unfortunately no longer to be found in all of them, it still survives in many thousands, adding an aura of moral dignity to their look of intelligence. Only the other day I read, once again, a report by a Gentile in which he describes not merely the Rembrandt-like features of such a Polish ghetto-face but particularly its saintly expression. How, then, could I be fearful of any threat to our fatherland if it were to admit Jews of this type?

Yet the reasons given for my plea on their behalf would admittedly be incomplete were I not to add my fervent hope that their

1. World War I.

coming might have an invigorating effect on our German Judaism and help raise its general level. For what good is it cautiously to conceal the fact that we are undergoing a continuous blood-letting? Nor will we be helped by the comforting thought that our best people do remain loyal to us. We need an infusion of fresh, undiluted blood. We must make provision for the future, for we have more than a mere inkling of the grave dangers threatening our distinct religious existence.

I for one have never glossed over the darker sides of East European Judaism. In fact, I have set German Judaism and its historical ideal as an example before Polish-Russian Jewry. But for this very reason I feel justified in emphasizing the new strength and support we might gain from an influx of East European Jews.

My acknowledgment of their virtues is by no means limited to an appreciation of the great intellectual vigor which makes many of these men shine at the academies of all countries. I recognize above all their sheer humaneness which has been enhanced and purified by their political martyrdom. There is probably no man among us who has not met and admired some Polish Jew of unsurpassed inner nobility.

No form of prejudice against the Jews hurts me as deeply—because none offends humanity in its purest form quite as badly—as the derision shown these people who bear the cross of the most wretched Jew-hatred. It is incomprehensible to me how one can revile these symbols of injustice on earth for their foibles and frailties, their squalor and destitution, rather than recognize, or at least sense, the nobility of soul (which has steeled their power of endurance) behind it all. This cruelty I must fight against, as a German and as a Jew.

I hope for the sake of my fatherland, and for the sake of my religion, that the traditional, the classical land of humanitarianism will not permit any closing of its borders to East European Jews even if the logic of our political situation were to suggest such a measure. Instead, I hope that these people will be admitted to the German Reich in recognition of their moral worth and their high cultural potential.

Ethical, political, and religious considerations alike merge in this hope of mine. Its fulfillment should yield a rich gain for the Jews of our fatherland too, ensuring the viability and continued existence of their religion and a more profound peace and closer harmony among them. For we shall be able to resolve our religious differences and reconcile our conflicts only to the extent to which we dedicate ourselves to the scientific study of our ancient religious sources and absorb their spirit. Therefore we must extend our welcome to those productive and active scholarly elements that still exist—a living tradition—in Eastern Europe.

Thou Shalt Not Go About as a Slanderer

Every Jew in the world knows—though he may not be consciously aware of it, much less act accordingly—that all Jews in the West (in contradistinction to those hailing from the East) have an intellectual as well as a psychological tie to Germany. Just as the Spanish Jews maintained and cultivated their beloved mother-tongue even in the Orient or wherever they found themselves after having been exiled, so the German Jews remained faithful to the German language even in the Crimea and other parts of Russia. Should not this linguistic phenomenon be indicative of some deep-seated affect in the hearts and minds of those whose wanderings have led them through German lands?

Not every Jew is aware of it, but every Jew ought to be: we owe the inner development that has led to the restructuring of our religion exclusively to Germany.

Moses Mendelssohn was a German man, a German thinker, and a German writer, on a par with and a genuine friend of the great Lessing.[1] It was Mendelssohn's German heart and mind that motivated him, another Luther, to translate the Pentateuch. Thus,

1. Gotthold Ephraim Lessing (1729–1781); German poet and philosopher of the Enlightenment.

he gave us access to the German language, enabling us to enter the world of general culture. And the entire inner rejuvenation of our religious services, incepted in Germany and by the German spirit, is the product of that German ethos and religiosity to which our own has always been akin. For the sense of history characteristic of Protestantism has also been a vital force in our own medieval philosophy of religion ever since Saadyah Gaon. The Reform of Judaism was a German Reform, reaching you from Germany and through Germans. Even those who do not accept this movement in some of its manifestations or who actually fight it are influenced by its spirit and have some relationship to it.

Moreover, the general cultural work Jews are engaged in everywhere has received special impetus from that German spirit which scholars who went from Germany to France, England, and Russia have transplanted in those countries. In fact, there is hardly an area of cultural endeavor anywhere in which German Jews have not achieved some degree of prominence. . . .

Dear brethren in America: you will now understand me when I say that any Jew of the West must, in addition to being loyal to his political fatherland, acknowledge, revere, and love Germany. For Germany is the motherland of his renewed religious spirit and his ingrained sense of aesthetics, and thus the center of all that has molded him culturally.[2]

2. See "The German and the Jewish Ethos I."

CHAPTER 7

Reconciliation

Editor's Note

The concept of reconciliation, Cohen holds, is so basic to man's sense of ethics that its rudiments can be traced back to a very early stage in the development of religion. As soon as he becomes conscious of the fundamental difference between his own being and that of the divinity, man also becomes conscious of a schism within himself: no longer at one with his God, he feels at odds with himself. Subsequently, he experiences a threefold sense of alienation reflected in the way he relates himself to God, his fellow man, and even to himself.

The Hebrew prophets emphasize, and by this emphasis hope eventually to resolve, the religious, social, and psychological conflicts resulting from man's feeling of alienation. Pointing out the moral futility of the sacrificial cult, they try to awaken in the people an understanding of the true nature of God and therefore of His demands for their conduct.

With this new understanding goes a growing awareness of the true nature and meaning of sin. Once man realizes that a God who is all justice and love asks man for nothing but justice and love, he also realizes that sin constitutes not so much a ritual as a moral transgression. God does not command to be worshipped by this or that rite; He demands to be served by a life of righteousness.

The unrighteous man who commits a wrong against another man therefore commits a wrong against God, and his reconciliation with God can only follow his reconciliation with his fellow man. Social justice in all its ramifications for the individual and society is thus the precondition for all reconciliation—with one's God, one's fellow man and, by implication, with oneself.

But before the prophets can teach their people this threefold meaning of reconciliation, they must demolish the ancient "mythic-tragic" notion of "family-engendered"—that is, inherited—guilt, or guilt by fate. The prophetic insight that no man is congenitally burdened with the sins of his fathers (nor, conversely, safeguarded against sin by their virtues) but that the individual, and he alone, is responsible for his acts and will be held accountable for his good or evil ways represents, to Cohen, a tremendous advance in religious thinking. It also leads to the development of the concept of repentance.

Man is born with a potential for good; but he may fall short of fulfilling that potential, owing to certain moral inadequacies that are part of the human condition. Either by inadvertence or because of poor judgment he may stray from the right path and go wrong. Self-purifying remorse, however, or a soul-searching act of genuine repentance will redeem him from his own evil inclinations so that he can correct his errors and return to the ways of God, that is, the ways of righteousness.

Reconciliation, repentance, and redemption are the keynotes sounded on the Day of Atonement, that singular day in the life of the Jew which frees as well as nourishes his own innermost resources, and "creates and keeps alive in him an inexhaustible source of strength: Jewish religiosity."

The Concept of Reconciliation

The concept of reconciliation, operative in the three major cultural areas of religion, art, and juridical as well as national ethics, exerts a threefold influence upon man: it affects his relations to God, his fellow man, and himself. Yet such a division is purely theoretical; in practice, the task of reconciliation demands man's efforts on all levels of his life at once. Therefore we see that even at the very beginnings of mankind's cultural development a rudimentary ethics assists religion in its effort to work out the problem of tragedy [posed by man's sense of alienation]. In fact, primitive religion, as yet closely linked to art, can be traced to and reflects that elemental sense of ethics which characterizes all three aspects of reconciliation.

There is an inner connection between the development of Greek religion and that of the so-called Orphic theology which, in turn, is not free of oriental speculation. In the earliest stages of Israelite as well as Greek history, the concept of reconciliation is still unknown. Just as the Greeks of that period are given to an unrestrained pursuit of pleasure and joy before their gods, so the Israelites' early cult indicates their enjoyment not merely before their God but also along with Him. The ensuing sacrificial rites had their origin not in any wish to reconcile, with a gift and as a sign of repentance, some mythological godhead that had been angered by some human wrongdoing. The sacrificial cult originated in man's naive sense of community with his gods. The earliest form of sacrifice is a meal consumed in the spirit in which members of a family or tribe might eat together. These sacramental meals are characterized not by a mood of renunciation but by an ostentatious lavishness, as a demonstration of man's vigor and prosperity. At best, they serve the purpose of including God in the mythic bond they establish among the participants; thus, they give rise to the concept of a covenant. But no thought of reconciliation is as yet directed towards this God with whom and not to whom one offers sacrifices. Man, not yet at odds with himself, still feels at one with his God. Only as he becomes aware of a schism within his own being does he experience a sense of separation from God as a Higher Being; and only as he discovers this Higher Being does he recover within himself his lost sense of unity.

It is the prophets who awaken man's awareness of a conflict within himself; yet this conflict is not the primary target of their moral indignation. In their zealous exhortations against the injustices rampant in all institutions of public life, they attempt to emphasize the conflict between man and man. This leads them to attack the people's sacrificial cult. Amos is not at all concerned with a possibly faulty performance of the sacrificial rites; he lashes out against the inner contradiction of such a form of worship. True worship of God, he says, manifests itself in man's entire conduct. Obviously, there is a glaring contrast between this new view of religious worship and all sacrificial practices. And when, prompted by fear, those later take the bloody form of renunciatory offerings, the embittered prophets grow ever more zealous. In contradistinction to the notion held so far that an evil power is part of the godhead's nature, they develop a truly mature concept of a God who is not merely omnipotent but acts out of justice and love and in turn asks for nothing but justice and love. The One God demands no so-called divine worship but solely and exclusively righteousness and morality.

The prophets' opposition to sacrifices is based on the moral idea of the Ten Commandments which center around the Sabbath law, the cornerstone of social ethics: ". . . so that thy man-servant and thy maid-servant may rest, as well as thou" (Deuteronomy 5:14). The Decalogue does not mention any sacrifice to be brought on the Sabbath nor indeed any sacrificial cult whatsoever. But the prophet's concept of God, though incompatible with the notion of ritual guilt, presently leads to the disclosure of a new sin and a new atonement, and thus to the development of monotheism's notion of reconciliation.

This notion emerges from the insight that man's relationship to his fellow man is frequently characterized by injustice and that a wrong committed against man constitutes a wrong committed against God. Reconciliation with the new, the true God can therefore come about only when envy and hatred are eliminated. For these are alienating vices that tear the individual apart and divide him into two souls or conflicting inclinations; but reconciliation with his fellow man will lead man to reconciliation with himself. And through these two modes of reconciliation the prophetic concept of man's reconciliation with God is realized.

From a historical perspective, however, it may easily be seen why this radical prophetic concept of reconciliation could not be fully accepted by a people whose great religious advance during the Exile—along with that of their prophets—was still accompanied by a lively interest in the priestly cult. But it would be unhistorical to regard this cult-orientation only as an impediment to the realization of the prophetic concept of morality. An unbiased examination of the facts will show us the light as well as the dark side of this particular development in prophetic thinking, whose first proponent is the priest and prophet Ezekiel. He clarifies a certain basic aspect of reconciliation which had remained somewhat ambiguous even in the Decalogue.

The second commandment states: ". . . for I, the Lord God, am a jealous God, visiting the iniquities of the fathers upon the children unto the third and fourth generation of them that hate me. . . ." Jewish tradition, in accordance with the Talmud, interprets this to mean: ". . . if they take up the deeds of their fathers with their own hands." Moreover, the translation "of them that hate me" must be considered wrong within the context of the commandment, as evidenced by the subsequent statement: ". . . and showing mercy unto the thousandth generation of them that love me" (Exodus 20:5;6). Love unto the thousandth generation, but punishment not beyond the fourth: this should surely show that the true God is the God of love. Nevertheless, it must be admitted that we have here still a trace of that thinking which establishes a connection between the individual's conduct and the fate of his progeny, and that this statement is indeed reminiscent of the mythic-tragic idea of family-engendered guilt and suffering. Taken over from antiquity even by a more recent age, this primitive concept ought to be wholly eradicated.

But to return to our historical survey: in Jerusalem, there had already existed an old saying that "the fathers have eaten sour grapes, and the children's teeth are set on edge" (Ezekiel 18:2). Now Ezekiel argues passionately that the son does not suffer on account of his father's conduct nor the father on account of his son's; the evil son of a righteous father will not prosper, and the good son of an evil father will fare well. "The soul that sinneth, it shall die" (Ezekiel 18:4). This idea is fundamental to any ethics of personal responsibility, and an understanding of this idea represents the most significant progress in the entire development of the concept of reconciliation.

The soul, that means the person, the individual. And it is his personality, his individuality which distinguishes man so that he is more than a mere link in the chain of generations. By defining sin as personal misconduct, Ezekiel discovered the concept of the moral individual. Though conducive to a life of virtue, this concept could not have been discovered through a life of virtue. The words "the soul that sinneth" imply a great ethical insight. For inasmuch as it is the individual who commits a sin, it is also the individual, the person, the soul who can muster that strength and gain that inner freedom which are the prerequisites of morality.

The man responsible for so far-reaching a reform of the people's ethics was also the originator of that sacrificial cult whose performance in the Temple was a state function in ancient Judaism. This fact should serve as a starting point for Bible criticism. True, from then on the place, time, material, and execution of any sacrifice were determined in the most minute ceremonial detail. True, too, the sacrificial rite was thereafter apt to appear to be the main concern of religion. Yet these strict regulations also impressed upon man the idea that his relationship to God must not be left to some festive hour of celebration or chance event in his personal life, but that it must become a constant component and an integral part of his existence. Sin seeks atonement through a sacrifice to God. These sacrificial rites, therefore, were intended to develop man's moral sense, and to awaken in him, as a precondition for moral conduct, an understanding of the nature of sin.

Hence, we find, in addition to the new sacrificial rites, a new kind of divine worship as still another means of deepening man's ethical awareness. It would seem that around this time prayers were introduced in the form of psalms, giving vent to the most profound emotions of the human heart. Man's heart knows no greater conflict than that caused by doubt, that is, by the suspicion that his belief in the superior power of the good may be nothing but delusion and that all hope in the eventual triumph of truth may, in the end, prove vain. It is here that prayer can enable us to scale the heights of moral confidence and trust; for God is the rock to which all hope must cling. Yet the struggle of the two souls within us, the realistic, skeptical soul and the soul which believes that the idea is realizable after all—this, too, constitutes prayer.

Polytheism does not know this kind of prayer (though, to be

sure, no historical system is quite so rigid as to exclude completely all seminal traces of other systems). The Greek built his temple not for the sake of worshipers—whom it could not have accommodated—but for an idol. And the Greek chose among his gods, selecting the one to whom a particular prayer might be addressed most suitably.

Monotheism, however, had always realized that such considerations must destroy all sense of sanctity. And now it also came to realize that the multiplicity of temples and temple-courts dedicated to the celebration of sacrificial rites was detrimental to the development of an inner sense of unity in man. The goal of prayer, however, is just such a unity of soul. Thus the injunction against any cult on the high places by those then in charge of religious legislation, and the restriction of the sacrificial cult to Jerusalem, may well represent the first step in the direction of that goal.

To be sure, this undertaking was motivated not only by religious but also by patriotic sentiments, namely, the exiles' longing for their home and country. Yet there were implications too for a certain growing inclination to dispense with sacrificial practices altogether; for during the Exile, the people's assemblies took place on the Sabbath and they were worship services only, without sacrifice. The fact, therefore, that any sacrificial rite would from now on be regarded as idol-worship if it were celebrated anywhere but in Jerusalem's Temple seems indicative of a tendency to give up that pagan notion which equated worship with sacrifice.

With this new orientation, the prophets of the Exile strove for a restoration of the centralized state on the basis of a centralized cult. At the same time, they once again took up their fight against a priestly aristocracy they could not dislodge. But this merely lent added support to their basic request: "Ye shall be unto Me a kingdom of priests, and a holy nation" (Exodus 19:6). This challenge to the people to become priest-like tended to obliterate any distinction between priest and layman. In fact, the organization of a priestly cult bore within itself the seeds of its own dissolution. An essential factor in all of this was the development of the Messianic idea which called all nations to a new service of God. Concomitantly, Jerusalem, given a new dimension as the focal point of

204   REASON AND HOPE

monotheistic mankind, lost its significance as a geographical local-
ity: "For My house shall be called a house of prayer for all peoples" (Isaiah 56:7).

According to the Talmud, there were to be seventy burnt offerings for the seventy nations. This interaction between Messianism
and the laws that regulated the sacrificial cult served to deempha-
size that particularism of national unity which was supposed to be
strengthened by the establishment of a central ceremonial location.
And thus, a new fundamental concept eme ged; for while the original intent of the new legislation had been the restoration of the
people, its actual result was the creation of a community (Gemeinde). God's community is not merely a special union of the
faithful, set apart from others. In the prophetic vision it was rather
a union of men across all barriers of class and nation, acting as if
with one conscience and constituting one moral mankind.

What actually was most objectionable in the entire official sacrificial institution was the priest himself representing a rank or caste;
this held particularly true for the High Priest and his political
power. But here, too, a circumstance that seemed at first to hinder
the free development of a sense of morality in the individual proved
instead to be of invaluable help. For inasmuch as the priest alone
offered the sacrifice, the individual on whose behalf he acted could
stay completely in the background and, in fact, did not even have
to be present. And this may well have been a contributing factor
in the gradual realization that there was no necessary connection
between sin and sacrifice.

The priest was not merely a priest but also a physician and public supervisor of the important hygienic measures which eventually
accompanied the sacrificial cult. Having always functioned as a
judge, the priest now took over, though in a new form, the office of
a criminal judge, thus fulfilling a negative rather than an absolving
function. In his capacity as judge, the priest symbolized the purpose of all punishment: correction and reconciliation. The secular
court was not abolished. However, this did not mean that the
priest-judge served merely as a surrogate for the criminal judge in
cases involving transgressions against any sacral hocus-pocus. On
the contrary: from the ceremonial as performed by the priest-judge

there now evolved a notion indicative of a heightened moral aware-ness—the concept of *shegaga,* the inadvertently committed sin.

Shegaga does not imply ignorance of the law but lack of intent. It is a concept that probably goes back to, or grew out of, a situa-tion in which the perpetrator of a given crime was not known. Ac-cording to ancient belief, the place where such a crime had oc-curred was to be purified. And there are indications in the Penta-teuch that *shegaga* meant, at first, such a purification. But even-tually the notion of *shegaga* also implied the establishment of places of sanctuary for someone who had unintentionally become a murderer; and this led gradually to a third stage in the develop-ment of this concept.

First, then, *shegaga* means a sin was committed secretly, without the community's knowledge. Secondly, it means an unintentionally committed sin which weighs upon man's conscience though he has no real reason for self-accusation. But only at the third stage, which reflects an increasing enlightenment, can the conscience-stricken individual experience any real relief from his anxiety. For here it is asked: are not all sins more or less unintended, viewed from a higher perspective? Is not every man's moral awareness more or less obscured by passion, or simply not highly enough de-veloped so that he has, as it were, no real freedom of choice?

These deliberations are admittedly two-edged and could lead to self-indulgence and irresponsibility. Yet they also represent the thinking of a Socrates—with whom all reasoned ethics starts—and no less that of prophetic religion. Here, it is true, God stands for law and justice; but He stands also, and quite as much, for love and reconciliation. Justice demands punishment; love demands rec-onciliation. This would indicate a contradiction not only within prophetic religion but even within God's own nature were it not for the overriding consideration that any transgression, no matter how punishable, is also only an error, and as such pardonable. Yet no human court of justice is competent to hand down an annulment of guilt such as the concept of *shegaga* implies. Such a revision of judgment is outside the province of human justice and can only come from on high. And the public performance of sacrificial rites evidently played an important role in demonstrating the profound meaning of this new moral concept and even of the God-idea itself.

The interpretation of *shegaga* as a sin which is the inevitable result of human frailty had to be augmented by another vital religious principle lest man succumb to the danger of self-extenuation. In the same Chapter 18 in which Ezekiel presents his view of individual guilt and individual virtue, he also teaches us the prerequisite for all human righteousness: repentance.

The Hebrew term for repentance, *teshuvah,* means "turning"— a turning from evil, a re-turning to the good, or a turning inward, into oneself. The originator of the sacrificial cult thus implicitly proclaims that an act of repentance is the decisive precondition of all religious services and all morality.

Here, we come to a fundamental problem of pure ethics, namely, man's reconciliation with himself. If the individual were to or had to see his own mistakes merely as weaknesses of his nature, he would neither be responsible for his own actions nor would he be aware of himself as a moral being. He can gain and maintain such an awareness, if indeed he wants to, only by a willing acceptance of his own accountability. The Biblical metaphor of the sinner's return from his accustomed ways is truly illuminating. For repentance does not begin with a comfortable kind of regret that takes absolution for granted; it begins with a re-turn. The term "way(s)," however, signifies even more. It is a summing-up of actions or conduct, as in "the ways of God" or "the way of man." For repentance is not limited to an isolated occurrence in man's life. It is based on an examination of his individual acts in the context of all willing and all doing; as an attitude, it controls the totality of man's being. Thus, repentance serves as a guidepost to a principled way of life, a life of integrity. Renewal of the entire human being—a new heart and a new mind—that is the true significance of repentance.

Repentance, then, represents the religious task of achieving moral awareness. . . .

Once man has searched the depths of his heart and true repentance has given him new strength for his moral struggles, a narrow moralist might feel that any further scruples would merely amount to self-torture or lead to self-defeating romantic notions. Yet such a shallow moralism is in no way representative of the profound insights of ethics. To assume that religion alone can make us aware of the limitations of human virtue is to misjudge ethics. True, the principle that man's reason is the source of all moral law is basic to ethics. Yet ethics also expresses the idea and proceeds on the assumption that all human virtue is inadequate and that all moral laws must therefore be and remain tasks solvable only in various degrees of approximation.

At this point, then, religion and ethics do not differ. Their real difference lies elsewhere: religion regards the idea of human inadequacy as the very premise of its existence. In the view of religion, therefore, morality cannot be self-revealed, that is, revealed by the human mind; it must be revealed by God. Hence, religion sees the reconciliation of man with man or of man with himself as a corollary of man's reconciliation with God. This view constitutes a grave danger; for it can be too narrowly interpreted and would then prove conducive to an indulgence in pious fantasies rather than to the promotion of good works. But it has also a truly positive aspect and is in fact responsible for the universal, moral impact of religion. For reconciliation with God means, to the genuinely religious man, not so much a replenishing of his strength as an acknowledgment of his weakness: seeking reconciliation, he declares his own finiteness. . . .

In Jewish thought, God's grace is the correlate of man's weakness. The bestowal of that grace is not tied to any particular event, and any mediation between God and man is not merely rejected, but is rejected as nonsensical. God's grace is fully manifest in His relationship to man, a direct relationship for which no mediator is needed. God's immediacy furnishes the ground for all redemption and reconciliation. God is love, and no specific demonstration is needed to communicate that love. Man, in turn, has only to repent and follow up his repentance with the right kind of conduct to partake of divine grace. The idea of love precludes any mediator. And the Jewish concept of man and his relation to God is quite incompatible with the concept of a mediator. Moreover, God's immediacy postulates man's unmediated, autonomous morality.

At this point of our deliberations, we must remember the influence which the institution of sacrifical rites exerted even upon this innermost development of the Jewish religion. As we said before, man withdraws behind the priest during the sacrificial rite; and so, in a manner of speaking, does God. It is the priest who offers the sacrifice and performs the act of expiation. And since this procedure is not conducive to the establishment of a relationship between man and God, the Israelite comes to divest himself of any notion that God might be his partner at the sacrificial offering. He faces only the priest who assists him, in a pagan-human way, to feel a sense of renunciation, gratefulness, and remorse. But God has no part in any of this. God enters into an immediate relationship to man only as man becomes aware of the meaning of repentance. The Bible speaks of the priest alone but never of God as the expiator at the sacrificial rite. And the Yom Kippur service is dominated not by the concept of *shegaga* alone but by the additional motto: "For on this day atonement shall be made for you, to cleanse you; from all your sins, before the Lord shall you be clean" (Leviticus 16:30). Not God but the High Priest brings about this atonement. But it is God before whom the act of cleansing takes place, and it is God to whom all striving for purity and all repentance are directed. He is the God of love—a love that does not have to be aroused or earned by any sacrifice. Nor does a sacrifice offer satisfaction to divine justice. God is, so to speak, completely latent during the sacrificial celebration which is wholly a function of the priest.

The growing awareness that the priestly act of cleansing merely symbolizes man's own purification before God enhances the individual's own moral efforts. Man begins to see that he cannot become pure through a priestly sacrifice but only before God, that is, through his own solemn striving for purity. Through such striving, man establishes his relationship to God, and God becomes his ideal. The Mishnah formulates Judaism's awareness of its world-historic truth by saying: "Blessed are ye, o Israel. Before whom are ye made clean and who makes you clean? Your Father in heaven . . ." (*Mishnah Yoma* 8:9). Purity before God can be achieved only through self-purification. In the Torah too, the commandment to be holy is subsequent to the injunction for self-sanctification: "Sanctify yourselves therefore, and be ye holy" (Leviticus 11:44; 20:7).

Maimonides views the entire ceremonial law under this aspect, and the history of the sacrificial cult proves him completely right. The sacrificial cult came to an end, one might say, because it had outlived its own validity and not because the Temple had been destroyed. Today, the memory of the sacrificial cult lingers on in our prayers like an echo of an ancient tale from our national past. In contradistinction, Christianity has made the idea of sacrifice basic to all reconciliation. There, God offers Himself up so as to redeem man. Mass as well as communion center around this divine sacrifice and thus represent the most important part of all Christian worship service. Our worship service, by contrast, is based on faith in the God of love, the God whose very essence is love and who is far beyond any human notion of sacrifice.

As his disciples sit mourning around the smouldering Temple ruins, Rabbi Johanan ben Zakkai tells them that even though they no longer possess an altar they still have loving deeds to perform. And he asks not for a restoration of the altar but for permission to establish an academy in Jabne. Thus, teaching and repentance supersede sacrificial rites. It was on the Day of Atonement, the day of reconciliation, that Moses descended from Mount Sinai with the second set of tablets. Reconciliation, this seems to say, is the express purpose of all teaching. In fact, we must apply our entire intellectual energy to the study of our teachings. "The study of the Torah surpasses all good works" (*Mishnah Peah* 1:1). The Torah constitutes God's communication to man, for man's reason is of divine origin. "The breath of the Almighty giveth them understanding" (Job 32:8).

In accordance with this statement, Ibn Ezra and Maimonides could say: "Reason is the mediator between man and God." Therefore, there need be no conflict between faith and reason, or science. "The world rests on three things: Torah, worship of God—which means repentance—and loving deeds" (*Abot* I:2). Torah and repentance are the sources from which loving deeds flow. We have no priest. Today, the Jewish home represents, as it were, the place of expiation. When the family, devoted to each other in love and respect and imbued with a sense of charity gather around the table, that table becomes the Jewish altar.

The Day of Atonement

Man has both the capacity and need for reconciliation with God. He has been created with a potential for good, and his every effort must be bent upon accomplishing that good. Yet there is not only good in man but also evil, just as there is not only truth in the world but also falsehood. Man's finite endeavors may be swayed by the influence of evil, and his finite intellect may fall prey to the lures of falsehood. But though he be susceptible to evil and error— for inadequacy and finiteness are part of the human condition— man is not evil by nature, that is, not by divine intent. But inasmuch as human and divine being can never be identical,[1] human nature can be neither entirely good nor entirely true. Even so, goodness and truth constitute man's task as well as his ultimate goal. Though he may indeed go wrong, man is not innately evil; he always remains a creature of God, who is the Originator and Guarantor of the good on earth.

These are some of the basic premises of absolute monotheism. And it is absolute monotheism alone that could have developed the idea of redemption in as pure a form as represented by the Day of Atonement, this epitome of Judaism. We might well paraphrase a verse in Deuteronomy [2] and ask: "Where is there another people that has a Day of Atonement?" And if any historical proof were still needed to show that the Pharisees are the authentic if one-

1. See "Uniqueness Rather Than Unity of God."
2. "For what great nation is there, that hath God so nigh unto them, as the Lord our God is whensoever we call upon Him?" (Deuteronomy 4:7).

sided successors of the prophets, that proof has been provided by the institution of the Day of Atonement. For the Pharisees, those sages of the Talmud, gave a new meaning to that Biblical day of the High Priest's sacrifice and thus virtually created the Day of Atonement—a wonderful consequence of monotheistic thinking.

But why a special Day of Atonement? Should not all of life be dedicated to the idea of reconciliation? This question can best be answered by a counter-question: why any special celebration at all or any particular worship service? Should not all of life be a continuous service of God?

It should indeed; and it is precisely this acknowledgment which constitutes the meaning of any religious rite and the significance of any symbolic celebration or religious service. A ritual merely serves as a symbol; it holds an image before man and sets up an ideal for him. And if this is true for any ritual, it is particularly true for the Day of Atonement, that exemplary day which is the very symbol of temporality as such.

Man, as mentioned before, has been created with a potential for good, for the actualization and advancement of that good. He is not fatefully enthralled by evil, though in his finiteness he cannot completely avoid it. He is capable of reconciliation with God and will in fact achieve it if only he strives for it with all his heart and mind. The Yom Kippur frees as well as nourishes man's innermost resources, creating and keeping alive in him an inexhaustible source of strength: Jewish religiosity.

Man strives for reconciliation with God—could he aspire to anything higher? Since identity with God is a paradoxical notion, reconciliation with Him remains man's only goal because it represents no less than his redemption from the conflicting forces within his own nature. Hence, reconciliation is more than a mere redemption from past sins; it overcomes sin or sinfulness by making man realize that the good in him can conquer his evil inclinations.

While reconciliation with God means man's redemption from the sinfulness which is his alleged nature, it does not mean a redemption from his finiteness nor from his human fate. Such an interpretation would reflect the errors of pantheism. The monotheistic concept of redemption neither belittles nor euphemizes man's this-worldly, sensate existence. It does not catapult man into a beyond that is expected to provide him with some consolation for his otherwise unalleviated suffering; nor does it relieve him from the routine of his everyday existence. In short, it does not exempt him from the here-and-now of life with its duties and hopes; it merely saves him from the allegation that he is in the unbreakable grip of evil. Or, to put it differently: man's redemption from sin in no way signifies a redemption from or suspension of his human condition; it signifies his reconciliation with God. And that, in turn, means that the breach between man and God is healed, but that their difference is in no way dissolved into identity.

The Day of Atonement is a banner day for monotheistic mankind. It stresses the fact that man not only has the capacity to aspire to reconciliation with God but that he is man only because of this capacity. And God's most profound significance consists in His power to grant this reconciliation to man. Hence, reconciliation is characteristic of God's very nature. Love and justice would be contradictory divine attributes were it not for the concept of reconciliation. The psalm speaks of God as "good and forgiving." What could be meant by God's goodness if not His readiness to grant forgiveness and reconciliation?

Monotheism has drawn some important and inescapable conclusions from its insight into God's nature. First, no one but God, the One and Only, can effectuate reconciliation. Secondly, even God in His mercy can bring about reconciliation only for that individual who, consciously striving for the good, recognizes sin for what it is and tries to liberate himself from it. Without my own moral effort and repentance even God cannot redeem me. The One and Only God has given me my share of the good; it is, therefore, incumbent upon me to rid myself of my share of evil. And, finally, the third conclusion: neither reconciliation nor redemption means that man will be released from his this-worldly, finite existence. Rather than create illusions and phantasmagoria, these concepts set up ideals for the moral work of mortal beings. Redemption has nothing to do with death or the beyond; man is not redeemed from life on earth with all its pain and suffering but merely from his errors and mistakes.

The Day of Atonement follows the "Day of Judgment" which ushers in the New Year. This designation, however, does not denote a "Last Judgment" but rather a divine judgment of all earthly existence. The Day of Judgment symbolizes God's daily judgment of "all the orders of creation," as one of the hymns of this day so beautifully puts it.

Divine judgment, reconciliation and redemption—the three together comprise one concept which epitomizes Judaism's absolute monotheism. In the Mishnah, there is a statement by Rabbi Akiba, as yet unsurpassed by any system of ethics: "Blessed are ye, o Israel. Before whom are ye made clean and who makes you clean? Your Father in heaven" (*Mishnah Yoma* 8:9).

CHAPTER 8

The Enduring Relevance
of Judaism

Editor's Note

Among the abiding values of Judaism is its central concern with ethics, which Cohen illustrates by juxtaposing the Aristotelian and Jewish ideals of selfhood. The former is typified by the solitary thinker, the latter by the individual engaged in social action. Only as one man relates himself to another does he become a truly human being, an "ethical self." Ethical interaction between I and Thou is as essential to the individual's sense of selfhood as it is for a meaningful life of society. Beyond that, it is indispensable for the eventual attainment of Judaism's most cherished goal: a world community of men united by a feeling of oneness through which they bear witness to the unique Oneness of God.

Judaism's idea of a "Messianic mankind" is but a corollary of its idea of God's Oneness, and both are timeless. They imbue man with a world-historical perspective, providing nations as well as individuals with the ideological and moral tools to cope with their political and moral problems.

An examination of these and other basic Jewish concepts yields an answer to the question about the continued relevance of the Jewish religion. Cohen finds that the uniquely One God of Judaism's absolute monotheism represents an idea which has lost none of its significance since its inception. And the Jewish tenet of God's absolute immateriality is as much of a prerequisite for all rational religious thought and all rational religious truth today as it was in the past and will be in the future. In fact, the future of "the moral universe" is bound up with man's recognition that God's spirituality makes it incumbent upon him to spiritualize his own life.

In Judaism, however, there can be neither spiritualization nor inspiration without knowledge. Knowledge leads to understanding, and understanding to action. To know God can only mean to understand His moral commandment and carry it out. But contemporary man does not yet fully understand this commandment, let alone carry it out. Modern culture has yet to cultivate "a concern for morality" and is still in dire need of religious values. The insights of Judaism and its "knowledge of morality" have therefore still much to contribute to society, and Judaism's ethical-cultural validity is as yet undiminished.

I and Thou: Selfhood Through Ethical Action

It is an intriguing [Aristotelian] illusion that the solitary thinker, in his state of eudaemony,[1] is most likely to attain full selfhood. We [Jews] know, however, that the isolated self exclusively engaged in thinking cannot be an ethical self. The ethical self must be engaged in action. For this self, there exists no I without a Thou. *Reah* means "the other," the one who is like you. He is the Thou of the I. Selfhood is the result of an unending relation of I and Thou as well as its abiding ideal. True, the ideal remains the ideal, as the task [of ethical action] remains the task. But an ideal is an ideal only because and insofar as it asks to be emulated so that I may approximate it. And a task is a task only because I am charged with it, because it is incumbent upon me. By working at this task, I work on myself, toward my selfhood.

In short, selfhood ensues from the interaction between I and Thou.

1. See footnote, p. 79.

Judaism's Relevance for Modern Man

You make a fundamental mistake in your treatment of the Jewish question when you fail to deal with a certain religious issue which is absolutely crucial to the entire controversy, though this is never admitted. You should, for once, examine the question whether the Jewish religion is still relevant today—that is, whether it has anything to contribute to our contemporary and indeed to all future cultural life—or whether its significance lies solely in its past history, namely, in the alleged fact that it represents an early stage in the development of religion.

First, you must learn to understand what the concept of the uniquely One God means in terms of divine immateriality, and that absolute immateriality is the prerequisite for the genuinely rational truth of any religion. Then, you must learn to comprehend what this most objective ground of all religion, the rationality of the One-God concept, means in terms not only of this religion's objective truth but also in terms of the veracity of any personal religious credo; and finally, what the veracity of man's religious credo means with regard to his veracity in all intellectual and moral questions: then, and then only, will you be in a position to judge the cultural significance of Judaism.

The Jewish religion with its "Hear, oh Israel!" is still a living reality among you. Do not let any race-superstition blind you to the meaning of this historical miracle. And do not lightly dismiss the fact that the timeless idea of a Messianic mankind—this corollary of the idea of the One God—can imbue man's historical consciousness with a sense of inner direction. Keep in mind too that only a moral interpretation of history will, in the long run, enable man to solve even his political and national problems in all their ramifications.

The so-called Jewish question, then, concerns by no means merely one or another religion or nation. Its central issue is nothing less than absolute monotheism. And absolute monotheism ought to be the highest ideal for all religions and therefore for all nations: the ideal of pure religion. Neither the Enlightenment nor modern legislation has succeeded in removing from the Jews the burden placed upon them by the prejudice that they represent nothing but a foreign race. This prejudice can and will disappear only when the inherent worth of their religion is fully recognized.

The spirit informing pure religion is more akin to the German spirit than to that of any other people. Hence, we German adherents of Jewish monotheism place our trust in history, confident that our innermost kinship to the German ethos will be acknowledged ever more willingly and frankly. Sustained by this confidence, we shall thus go on as German men and German citizens and at the same time remain unshakably loyal to our Jewish religion.

Judaism's Significance for the Religious Progress of Mankind

1. We must try to comprehend the special character of monotheism. Here, [divine] unity means absolute, unique Oneness, implying a total distinctiveness [of divine being] from all other modes of being,[1] and not merely from material being but from all other spiritual being as well. It is this distinctiveness alone which imparts true spirituality to the unique being of the uniquely One God. From a universal point of view, this must admittedly seem to be a one-sided position; yet this one-sidedness is intrinsic to the Jewish concept of God. Inasmuch as God's being is distinct from all other being, He represents true being. All other being, whether nature's

1. See "Uniqueness Rather Than Unity of God."

or man's, would by comparison therefore be mere appearance or just a shadow, were it not for the capacity inherent in God's creature and image to give meaning and thus substance to this being.

Hence, the absolute spirituality of Jewish monotheism is akin to the philosophical concept of moral idealism. Before the idea of the One, the spiritual God all forces of nature and culture pale into insignificance, and all earthly being becomes incommensurable with the being of this spiritual God. The significance of the One God, therefore, cannot lie in His relation to nature or to man, for such a relationship presupposes commensurability. Or, expressed in positive terms: the significance of this monotheistic God-concept lies in that principle of spirituality in which the moral universe—in contradistinction to the world of nature—as well as all ethics are grounded.

Here, an objection will probably be raised: if God were to denote no more than the law and prototype of morality, religion would, by implication, simply dissolve into ethics; yet, the two are not supposed to be identical. But what actually can religion offer that goes beyond ethics? Ethics would be demeaned and religion obscured if God's significance were to be found beyond the realm of morality. The ethics intrinsic to God's nature, and that alone, constitutes religion in Judaism. God's essence is comprised of His attributes. And the so-called thirteen attributes refer exclusively to God's love and justice which make Him the prototype of human morality. All mystic speculations about any other aspects of His nature are rejected as potential violations of the fundamental principle of His unity and His unique Oneness.

The enthusiasm of Jewish religiosity stems from an awareness of the crucial importance of this principle. And this awareness, permeating all levels and degrees of human insight, is as alive in every Jew today as it has been at all times. To understand this, one must have experienced and observed the fervor with which the Jew prays the "Hear, oh Israel" at the conclusion of the Day of Atonement or with which he utters these words with his last breath as his soul leaves his body. It is the same sense of exultation expressed so beautifully by the psalmist: "Whom have I in heaven but Thee? And beside Thee I desire none upon earth" (Psalms

73:25); or: "But as for me, the nearness of God is my good" (Psalms 73:28).

One does not grasp the special character of this Jewish enthusiasm if one equates it with the mysticism of pantheism or with love of Christ. In both of these, man is akin to God. But the uniqueness of the Jewish God precludes any comparison with heaven or earth or any conjoining of God and man.

To be sure, pantheism cannot be regarded solely as an impediment to the development of religion. And far be it from us to imply that love of Christ as the ideal of mankind has not contributed much to religious progress. But it is well known that pantheism intrinsically poses a threat to the moral impact of the God-idea. And we are equally aware of the fact that Christianity itself, at different times, has been imperilled by a one-sided love of Christ.

The spirituality of Judaism's One God is evidenced by His incomparability to anything human whatsoever. Consequently, any mediation between God and man that a hypostatized human being might undertake is felt to be at variance with God's nature. And this brings us to the second factor characteristic of Judaism's contribution to man's religious progress.

2. The objective of religion as such is reconciliation. But the notion of man's reconciliation with God actually serves religion merely as an expedient in promoting its ethical concept of man's reconciliation with himself. Religion, however, would obliterate itself if it were to give up this indispensable means to its ultimate end—if, that is, it were to renounce the notion of or demand for man's reconciliation with God.

It is well known that ancient Biblical Judaism practiced pagan sacrificial rites, though it engaged in animal sacrifices only. The prophets' zeal against these practices suggests to historians the possibility that the inner development of Judaism might have led to a gradual abolition of those sacrificial rites even if the Temple had not been destroyed. Rabbi Johanan ben Zakkai, as is well known, did not ask Vespasian for the preservation of the Temple but for permission to establish an academy in Jabne. And of all the festivals of post-Biblical Judaism none bears out the above-mentioned theory better than the Day of Atonement, which remains the hall-mark and living symbol of modern Judaism.

On this one day, many Jews of our time seek to act out their sense of religious identity. They confess their sins which, conforming to Oriental custom, are enumerated painstakingly and minutely. But there is not a single mention of a breach of ritual law. Only moral transgressions, and they alone, are soul-searchingly reviewed.

The Jew needs no special divine arrangement, involving the very nature of God, to attain peace of mind through peace with God. In Judaism, no priest—as vicar of God—nor any God-man may say: I am the way to God. Here, the soul struggles without any mediator and is redeemed through its own repentance, through prayer, and through its resolve towards ethical conduct.

From this unmediated redemptive effort of man, directed to the God of morality, a great gain has accrued to theoretical ethics too: the concept of the unwittingly committed sin (*shegaga*).[2] The triumph of having achieved redemption culminates in the Socratic insight that all human conduct is characterized by weakness, by man's limited knowledge and his inadvertence. This is the motto proclaimed on the Day of Atonement: "And the congregation of Israel shall be forgiven, as well as the stranger that dwells among them, for they have all transgressed unwittingly."

3. Foremost among the preconceived notions which preclude any real understanding of Judaism is the one resulting from the erroneous translation of "Torah" as "Law" rather than "Teaching." The Pentateuch by no means commands merely love of God, for love of God could possibly be manifested by obeying His law. Rather, and to no less a degree, it demands knowledge of God. "Know this day, and lay it to thy heart . . ." (Deuteronomy 4:39). Love of God is love of morality. One cannot love God as one loves a human being. But to love spiritually means, simply and solely, to cultivate a concern for morality. Morality, however, even if it is not systematized in an ethical structure, presupposes knowledge. Torah therefore must mean instruction in and knowledge of morality.

2. See "The Concept of Reconciliation."

It may be one of the most telling phenomena of Jewish history that in the consciousness of the Jewish people the difference between poor and rich has never meant the difference between ignorance and education (or even scholarship), not even at times of great oppression and persecution.

The absence of a real proletariat among the Jews throughout their history, is, in the last analysis, due to the fact that religion (Torah) was never merely law but always living instruction. Though the poor worked hard at earning a living, they were no strangers to scholarly pursuits. At any comparatively free hour and especially late at night, they engaged in the study of the Talmud. Jewish literateness constitutes one of the most important elements of religious progress as such. This fact is little known though, and its great cultural and historical significance for Judaism's otherwise inexplicable survival is not sufficiently appreciated. . . .

Not merely knowledge of the Bible but also the study of the so-called oral tradition, the Talmud and all subsequent literature, filled the intellectual life of poor and rich alike. Even in our prayer we recite the Talmudic assertion that the study of our teachings surpasses the fulfillment of all other commandments. Hence, ignorance could never have been tolerated among the people.

By the same token, no professional clergy that would arrogate all learning to itself could come into being once the priestly hierarchy had been abolished. Nor could Jewish religious thought ever develop the notion that the most profound truths of religion are beyond intellectual comprehension and ought to be accepted on faith alone.

Within Jewish consciousness, there is no room for such an offensive dichotomy between faith and reason. Faith—the Hebrew term is derived from the root meaning "firmness"—is always supposed to be and is indeed required to be consonant with reason. It is God's essence alone which is considered beyond positive knowledge. His existence, however, is a matter of fervent faith based on clear understanding: an understanding of the nature of morality.

Through this interpretation of the meaning of Torah and through its practical application, the Mosaic injunction: "And ye shall be unto Me a kingdom of priests, and a holy nation" (Exodus 19:6) became a reality. And this fundamental principle was responsible not merely for the abolition of a clerical hierarchy; it had an impact too on the entire social structure of this community of faith and so affected its practical ethics.

4. Of the Ten Commandments, only the one dealing with the Sabbath underwent a marked change when the Decalogue was reiterated. In Exodus, the story of the creation itself explains why the Sabbath came into being: it is creation's final goal, representing, as such, surely more than a so-called "merely religious" motive. Nevertheless, Deuteronomy simply cancels out this explanation and replaces it with the great injunction: "Observe the sabbath day, to keep it holy . . . in it thou shalt not do any manner of work, thou, nor thy son, nor thy daughter, nor thy man-servant, nor thy maid-servant . . . And thou shalt remember that thou wast a servant in the Land of Egypt . . ." (Deuteronomy 5:12–15). Even if the Jewish religion had no other merits, its institution and preservation of the Sabbath law alone would have added a new dimension to the progress of religion as such.

The Sabbath, the very symbol of genuine religious and social progress, brought to the Jew of the medieval ghetto the solace of a cultural existence because it enabled him to live in accord with his basic religious principles. The entire intellectual structure of Judaism was kept alive only because this day, week after week, was given over not simply to physical rest from the workday routine nor solely to so-called worship services but equally to the study of the Torah. . . .

There can be no inspiration without instruction: this is the thought that underlies all worship in Judaism and, indeed, all its religious life.

The Spiritual Validity of Judaism

It is generally said that modern man ought to be above religion.
It is, however, not said what should be above modern man—what
he should recognize, or define, as the ultimate principle of his
being. If modern man is considered to be even above God, then
Judaism is indeed antiquated. But as long as we feel that the God-
idea is still valid for our modern culture, Judaism, too, is valid
still.

Sources for Quoted Texts

All quoted texts are taken from Volumes I–III of Hermann Cohen's *Juedische Schriften*, edited by Bruno Strauss, with introduction by Franz Rosenzweig, three volumes, Berlin, 1924. Most of this material appears in English translation for the first time.

Chapter 1 (pp. 42–61)
"Religious Postulates" (*Religioese Postulate*), 1907; I, pp. 1–14; excerpts.
"Love of Religion" (*Die Liebe zur Religion*), 1911; II, pp. 142–148.
"On Jewish Education," from *Emanzipation* [Emancipation], 1912; II, pp. 220–228; excerpts.
"The Transcendent God: Archetype of Morality," from *Die Religioesen Bewegungen der Gegenwart* [Religious Movements of Our Time], 1914; I, pp. 36–65; excerpt.

Chapter 2 (pp. 63–102)
"The Social Ideal As Seen by Plato and by the Prophets" (*Das soziale Ideal bei Platon und den Propheten*), 1916; I, pp. 306–330; excerpts.
"Affinities Between the Philosophy of Kant and Judaism" (*Innere Beziehungen der Kantischen Philosophie zum Judentum*), 1910; I, pp. 284–305; excerpts.
"Uniqueness Rather Than Unity of God" (*Einheit oder Einzigkeit Gottes*), 1917; I, pp. 87–99.

Chapter 3 (pp. 104–127)
"The Style of the Prophets" (*Der Stil der Propheten*), 1901; I, pp. 262–283; excerpts.
"On Messianism," from *Die Bedeutung des Judentums fuer den*

religioesen Fortschritt der Menschheit) [Judaism's Significance for the Religious Progress of Mankind], 1910; I, pp. 18–35; excerpts.

"The Messianic Idea" *(Die Messiasidee)*, c. 1890–92; I, pp. 105–139; excerpts.

Chapter 4 (pp. 129–160)

"Reason, the Hallmark of Divine Creation," from *Der Jude in der christlichen Kultur* [The Jew in a Christian Culture], 1917; II, pp. 193–209; excerpt.

"The Holy Spirit" *(Der heilige Geist)*, 1915; III, pp. 176–196.

"God's Nearness," from *Die Lyrik der Psalmen* [The Lyricism of the Psalms], 1914; I, pp. 237–261; excerpt.

"On the Aesthetic Value of Our Religious Education" *(Ueber den aesthetischen Wert unserer religioesen Bildung)*, c. 1914; I, pp. 211–236; excerpts.

"Trust in God" *(Gottvertrauen)*, 1916; I, pp. 100–104; excerpt.

Chapter 5 (pp. 161–171)

"An Argument Against Zionism," from *Antwort auf das offene Schreiben des Herrn Dr. Martin Buber an Hermann Cohen* [A Reply to Dr. Martin Buber's Open Letter to Hermann Cohen], 1916; II, pp. 328–340; excerpt.

"Religion and Zionism" *(Religion und Zionismus)*, 1916; II, pp. 319–327; excerpt.

Chapter 6 (pp. 173–193)

"The German and the Jewish Ethos I" *(Deutschtum und Judentum I)*, 1915; II, pp. 237–301; excerpts.

"The German and the Jewish Ethos II" *(Deutschtum und Judentum II)*, 1916; II, pp. 302–318; excerpts.

"On Closing the Borders" *(Grenzsperre)*, 1916; II, pp. 378–380.

"Thou Shalt Not Go About As a Slanderer" *("Du sollst nicht einhergehen als ein Verleumder")*, 1915; II, pp. 229–236; excerpt.

Chapter 7 (pp. 195–213)

"The Concept of Reconciliation" *(Die Versoehnungsidee)*, c. 1890–92; I, pp. 125–139; excerpts.

"The Day of Atonement" *(Der Tag der Versoehnung)*, 1917; I, pp. 140–144, excerpt.

Chapter 8 (pp. 215–226)

"I and Thou: Selfhood Through Ethical Action," from *Charakteristik der Ethik Maimunis* [A Critical Study of Maimonides' Ethics], 1908; III, pp. 221–289; excerpt.

"Judaism's Relevance for Modern Man," from *Betrachtungen*

ueber Schmollers Angriff [Reflections on an Attack by Schmoller], 1917; II, pp. 381–397; excerpt.
"Judaism's Significance for the Religious Progress of Mankind" (*Die Bedeutung des Judentums fuer den religioesen Fortschritt der Menschheit*), 1910; I, pp. 18–35; excerpts.
"The Spiritual Validity of Judaism," from *Salomon Neumann*, 1908; II, pp. 425–438; excerpt.

Further Reading

Cohen's major Jewish work appeared in English as *Religion of Reason out of the Sources of Judaism*, translated by Simon Kaplan and with an introduction by Leo Strauss (New York: Frederick Ungar Publishing Co., 1972.) The following is some selected secondary literature in English.

Books

Dietrich, Wendel S. *Cohen and Troeltsch: Ethical Monotheistic Religion and Theory of Culture*. Atlanta: Scholars Press, 1986.
Analyzes the dialogue between Cohen and the leading figure in German liberal Protestantism.

Kaplan, Mordecai M. *The Purpose and Meaning of Jewish Existence*. Philadelphia: Jewish Publication Society, 1964.
English rendition of contents of Cohen's *Religion der Vernunft* in epitomized form plus critical examination of its arguments and shortcomings owing to limitations of Cohen's time and place.

Kluback, William. *Hermann Cohen: The Challenge of a Religion of Reason*. Chico, CA: Scholars Press, 1984.
Explores Cohen's endeavor to join biblical faith with Kantian philosophy.

_____. *The Idea of Humanity: Hermann Cohen's Legacy to Philosophy and Theology*. Lanham, MD: University Press of America, 1987.
A set of neo-Kantian essays, some of which focus on Cohen, especially in relation to his contemporaries.

_____. *The Legacy of Hermann Cohen*. Atlanta: Scholars Press, 1989.
Essays dealing with various aspects of Cohen's thought, especially its social implications.

231

Melber, Jehuda. *Hermann Cohen's Philosophy of Judaism.* New York: Jonathan David, 1968.
Critical examination of Cohen's philosophy of Judaism from an Orthodox point of view.

Weiss-Rosmarin, Trude. *Religion of Reason: Hermann Cohen's System of Religious Philosophy.* New York: Bloch Publishing Co., 1936.
Cohen's philosophy of religion in the context of his total system of philosophy.

Articles and Essays

Agus, Jacob B. "Hermann Cohen," *Modern Philosophies of Judaism,* pp. 57–128. New York: Behrman House, 1941.

Altmann, Alexander. "Theology in Twentieth Century German Jewry," *Yearbook I of the Leo Baeck Institute,* pp. 193–216. London: East and West Library, 1956.

Bergman, Samuel Hugo. "Hermann Cohen: The Religion of Reason from the Sources of Judaism," in *Faith and Reason: An Introduction to Modern Jewish Thought,* trans. and ed. Alfred Jospe, pp. 27–55. New York: Schocken Paperback, 1963.

———. "Hermann Cohen," in *Between East and West: Essays Dedicated to the memory of Bela Horovitz,* ed. Alexander Altmann, pp. 22–47. London: East and West Library, 1958.

Berkovits, Eliezer. "Hermann Cohen's Religion of Reason," *Major Themes in Modern Philosophies of Judaism,* pp. 1–36. New York: Ktav Publishing House, 1974.

Dietrich, Wendell S. "The Function of the Idea of Messianic Mankind in Hermann Cohen's Later Thought." *Journal of the American Academy of Religion* 48 (June 1980): 245–58.

Fackenheim, Emil. *Hermann Cohen—After Fifty Years,* The Leo Baeck Memorial Lecture No. 12. New York: Leo Baeck Institute, 1969.

Fischoff, Ephraim. "Hermann Cohen," in *Great Jewish Thinkers in the Twentieth Century,* ed. Simon Noveck, pp. 105–33. Washington, D.C.: B'nai B'rith, 1963.

Guttman, Julius. "Hermann Cohen," *Philosophies of Judaism,* pp. 400–416. New York: Anchor Books, 1966.

Jacob, Walter. "Hermann Cohen on Christianity," *CCAR Journal* 68 (January 1970): 61–69. New York: Central Conference of American Rabbis.

Jospe, Eva. "Hermann Cohen's Judaism: A Reassessment," *Judaism* 25 (Fall 1976): 461–72.

Nauen, Franz. "Hermann Cohen's Concept of the State and the Problem of Anti-Semitism (1867–1907)," *Jahrbuch des Instituts fuer deutsche Geschichte* 8 (1979): 257–82.

_____. "Hermann Cohen's Perceptions of Spinoza: A Reappraisal," *AJS Review* 4 (1979): 111–24.

_____. "Secularization and the Law: Ethical and Religious Values in the Thought of Hermann Cohen," *Jahrbuch des Instituts fuer deutsche Geschichte* 6 (1977): 311–35.

Novak, David. "Universal Moral Law in the Theology of Hermann Cohen," *Modern Judaism* 1 (May 1981): 101–17.

Rosenthal, Erwin I.J. "Hermann Cohen and Heinrich Graetz," *Salo Wittmayer Baron Jubilee Volume*, Vol.II, pp. 725–43. Jerusalem: American Academy for Jewish Research, 1974.

Rotenstreich, Nathan. "From the Ethical Idea to the True Being: Hermann Cohen," *Jewish Philosophy in Modern Times*, pp. 52–106. New York: Holt, Rinehart and Winston, 1968.

_____. "Hermann Cohen: Judaism in the Context of German Philosophy," in *The Jewish Response to German Culture: From the Enlightenment to the Second World War*, ed. Jehuda Reinharz and Walter Schatzberg, pp. 51–63. Hanover, NH: University Press of New England, 1985.

Schwarzchild, Steven S. "'Germanism and Judaism'—Hermann Cohen's Normative Paradigm of the German-Jewish Symbiosis," in *Jews and Germans from 1860 to 1933: The Problematic Symbiosis*, ed. David Bronsen, pp. 129–72. Heidelberg: Carl Winter Universitaetsverlag, 1979.

_____. "The Title of Hermann Cohen's 'Religion of Reason out of the Sources of Judaism,'" in *The Life of Covenant: The Challenge of Contemporary Judaism: Essays in Honor of Herman E. Schaalman*, ed. Joseph A. Edelheit, pp.207–20. Chicago: Spertus College of Judaica Press, 1986.

Slonimsky, Henry. "Hermann Cohen," in *Essays*, pp. 97–112. Cincinnati: Hebrew Union College Press; Chicago: Quadrangle books, 1967.

Weiss, Raymond L. "Hermann Cohen's 'Religion of Reason': History and Religious Liberalism," *CCAR Journal* 21 (Winter 1974): 55–60.

Index